# Everyday Mediterranean recipes in the air fryer.

## 30-Day Meal Plan: Easy, Fast, Tasty and Healthy Recipes. Stress-free cooking, start today

DRAKE SPRAGGINS

D1518531

# Table of Contents

Notice of Copyright

# INTRODUCTION

## Preface: Savoring the Mediterranean Breeze with an Air Grill

In the heart of the Mediterranean lies a world of culinary traditions shaped by the sun, the sea, and the land. This book, "Mediterranean Air Grill: Flavors of the Sun-Kissed Sea," is born from a desire to capture the essence of this rich culinary heritage and adapt it to the modern convenience of air grilling. As you turn these pages, you embark on a journey that marries the age-old flavors of the Mediterranean with the innovation of contemporary cooking techniques.

The inspiration for this book came from a simple realization: the vibrant, fresh, and diverse dishes of the Mediterranean region can be perfectly suited to the fast, healthy, and flavorful cooking methods offered by an air grill. With this appliance, the natural tastes and textures of Mediterranean ingredients are elevated, creating dishes that are both nourishing and tantalizing to the palate.

"Mediterranean Air Grill" is more than a cookbook; it's a passage to a new way of cooking and experiencing food. It introduces you to a method that retains the authenticity of Mediterranean cuisine while embracing the efficiency and health benefits of air grilling. Each recipe has been carefully crafted to ensure that it remains true to its roots, capturing the soulful and rustic flavors that are the hallmark of Mediterranean dishes.

The book is structured to guide you through the various landscapes of the Mediterranean, from the coastal towns of Italy and Greece to the spice-laden markets of North Africa and the Middle East. It showcases how the air grill can be used to its fullest potential, transforming simple ingredients like olives, tomatoes, fish, and grains into exquisite meals that speak of their origin.

Throughout this journey, you will discover that Mediterranean cooking is more than just a style of food; it's a way of life that celebrates the joy of sharing, the importance of community, and the pleasure of eating well. By integrating the air grill into this culinary tradition, we bring a touch of modernity to the table, making these timeless recipes more accessible and fitting for today's lifestyle.

As you delve into the recipes and stories contained within "Mediterranean Air Grill: Flavors of the Sun-Kissed Sea," you will find more than just instructions for cooking; you will uncover a new appreciation for the simplicity, healthfulness, and beauty of Mediterranean cuisine, all through the lens of air grilling. This book is an invitation to explore, to taste, and to celebrate the enduring allure of the Mediterranean kitchen, reimagined for the contemporary cook.

# AIR FRYER ESSENTIALS

## Introduction to Air Frying Mastery

The air fryer has revolutionized home cooking, offering a healthier alternative to traditional frying methods. Mastering air fryer techniques can elevate your cooking, ensuring crispy, evenly cooked meals every time. This chapter delves into the essential skills and tricks to harness the full potential of your air fryer, transforming you into an air frying aficionado.

Understanding Air Fryer Mechanics

Before diving into specific techniques, it's crucial to understand how an air fryer works. Unlike conventional ovens, air fryers circulate hot air around the food at high speed, cooking it quickly and evenly. This rapid air circulation creates a crisp outer layer, mimicking the results of deep-frying but with significantly less oil. Familiarity with your air fryer's settings and capabilities is key to optimizing its performance.

Preparation: The Key to Success

Proper preparation can make a significant difference in the outcome of your air-fried dishes. Here's what to keep in mind:

Dry Foods Well: Excess moisture can lead to soggy results. Pat foods dry before cooking to achieve maximum crispiness.
Use the Right Amount of Oil: While air frying requires less oil than traditional frying, a light coat can improve texture and flavor. Use an oil sprayer or brush to evenly coat the food.
Don't Overcrowd: To ensure even cooking, place food in a single layer, allowing space for air circulation. Cook in batches if necessary.
Temperature and Timing

Getting the temperature and timing right is essential:

Preheat the Air Fryer: Like an oven, preheating your air fryer can lead to better cooking results. A 3-5 minute preheat is usually sufficient.
Understand Timing: Cooking times can vary based on the food type and size. Start with recommended times in recipes, then adjust based on your preferences and appliance specifics.
Flip or Shake Regularly: To cook food evenly, flip larger items halfway through or shake the basket for smaller items like fries or vegetables.
Advanced Air Frying Techniques

To elevate your air frying game, consider these advanced techniques:

Layering: Use racks or skewers to layer food, increasing the cooking capacity and ensuring even air flow.
Breading and Coating: For a crispy exterior, lightly coat food with breadcrumbs or batter. Ensure the coating is dry and adheres well to prevent it from blowing off.
Combining Foods: Cook complete meals by combining proteins and vegetables in the air fryer. Balance cooking times by adding ingredients in stages, based on how long they take to cook.
Creative Uses of the Air Fryer

Beyond frying, your air fryer can bake, roast, and grill. Experiment with:

Baking: From muffins to small cakes, air fryers can be used for baking. Use air fryer-compatible bakeware to achieve the best results.
Roasting: Vegetables and meats roast beautifully in an air fryer, developing a flavorful, caramelized exterior.
Grilling: Get grill-like results by cooking meats or vegetables at high temperatures until you achieve the desired char.
Troubleshooting Common Issues

If you encounter problems, consider these tips:

Uneven Cooking: Rotate or flip food more frequently to ensure even exposure to the hot air.
Not Crispy Enough: Increase the temperature or cooking time slightly, but watch carefully to avoid overcooking.
Food Sticking: Use parchment paper with holes, or lightly oil the basket to prevent sticking.
Conclusion: Embracing the Air Fryer Lifestyle

With practice, you can master these techniques to make the most of your air fryer, creating delicious, healthy meals with ease. Remember, the key to air frying success is experimentation and adaptation, finding what works best for your tastes and appliance.

This chapter has equipped you with the knowledge and skills to become proficient in air frying, ensuring you can create a wide range of dishes that are both tasty and healthy. As you grow more comfortable with these techniques, you'll discover the true versatility and convenience of the air fryer in your culinary repertoire.

# Breakfasts

Mediterranean-Inspired Breakfasts on the Air Grill

Immerse yourself in the Mediterranean flavors with our breakfast creations, perfectly suited for the air grill. Each dish brings a taste of the sunny coastlines and vibrant markets of the Mediterranean right to your breakfast table.

Grilled Mediterranean Toast:
Savor the aroma of freshly grilled bread as it emerges golden brown and crispy from the air grill. Topped with creamy hummus or tangy tzatziki sauce, every slice becomes a canvas for a colorful mosaic of sliced tomatoes, cucumbers, and crumbled feta cheese. A harmonious blend of flavors and textures awaits, promising a delightful start to your day.

Crispy Air-Grilled Cereal Clusters:
Crispness fills the air as clusters of wholesome cereal, nuts, seeds, and dried fruits undergo their transformation on the air grill. Golden and fragrant, each bite is a symphony of crunch and sweetness, infused with the earthy richness of olive oil and the subtle sweetness of honey. Paired with velvety Greek yogurt, it's a breakfast that celebrates the simplicity and abundance of Mediterranean ingredients.

Fluffy Greek Yogurt Pancakes:
The gentle sizzle of batter hitting the hot grill fills the air, signaling the creation of fluffy pancakes with a Mediterranean twist. With each flip, the pancakes take on a golden hue, their texture light and airy, infused with the tangy richness of Greek yogurt. Topped with fresh berries and a drizzle of honey, they offer a decadent yet wholesome start to your morning, reminiscent of leisurely breakfasts overlooking the azure waters of the Mediterranean.

Transport yourself to the sun-drenched shores and bustling markets of the Mediterranean with our breakfast offerings for the air grill. Each dish embodies the spirit of the region, offering a tantalizing glimpse into its rich culinary heritage and vibrant flavors. Start your day with a taste of the Mediterranean and let its warmth and vitality infuse every bite.

# Breakfasts
## Toasts

### Classic Avocado Toast

*Prep: 5 min.    Cooking: 3-5 min.    Serves: 1-2*

*Instructions:*
1. Preheat the air fryer to 200°C (390°F).
2. Place the bread slices in the air fryer basket and cook for about 3 minutes, or until they are toasted to your liking.
3. In the meantime, mash the avocado and season with salt and pepper.
4. Spread the mashed avocado evenly on the toasted bread slices.

*Ingredients:*
1. 2 slices of your preferred bread
2. 1 ripe avocado
3. Salt and pepper to taste

*Calories: 200-250.    Fat: 15g    Carbohydrates: 20g   Protein: 5g    Fiber: 7g*

### Tomato Basil Toast

*Prep: 5 min.    Cooking: 5-7 min.    Serves: 1-2*

*Instructions:*
1. Preheat the air fryer to 200°C (390°F).
2. Place the bread slices in the air fryer basket and toast for about 3 minutes, or until lightly golden.
3. Arrange tomato slices on the toasted bread, and add a sprinkle of salt and pepper.
4. Return to the air fryer and cook for an additional 2-4 minutes, or until the tomatoes are slightly roasted.
5. Top with fresh basil leaves and a drizzle of olive oil before serving. Optionally, add cheese before the final air frying step for a melted topping.

*Ingredients:*
1. 2 slices of bread (such as whole grain or sourdough)
2. 1 large ripe tomato, sliced
3. Fresh basil leaves
4. Olive oil for drizzling
5. Salt and pepper to taste
6. Optional: mozzarella or Parmesan cheese, thinly sliced or grated

*Calories: 150-200    Fat: 4g    Carbohydrates: 20-25g   Protein: 5g    Fiber: 3-4g*

# Toasts

## Egg and Spinach Toast

*Prep: 5 min.     Cooking: 8-10 min.     Serves: 1-2*

*Instructions:*

1. Preheat the air fryer to 180°C (350°F).
2. Lightly toast the bread in the air fryer for 2-3 minutes, or until it is slightly crispy.
3. Sauté spinach in a pan with a bit of olive oil or butter until just wilted, then season with salt and pepper.
4. Place the wilted spinach on top of the toasted bread slices.
5. Create a small well in the center of the spinach and carefully crack an egg into each well.
6. Return the toast with spinach and egg to the air fryer and cook for 5-7 minutes, or until the egg whites are set and the yolks are cooked to your liking.
7. Optionally, sprinkle some shredded cheese over the toast before returning it to the air fryer..

*Ingredients:*

1. 2 slices of whole-grain bread
2. 2 large eggs
3. 1 cup fresh spinach leaves
4. Salt and pepper to taste
5. Optional: shredded cheese, olive oil, or butter for extra flavor and richness

*Calories: 250-300   Fat: 10-15g   Carbohydrates: 20-25g   Protein: 15-20g.   Fiber: 4-5g*

## Smoked Salmon Toast

*Prep: 5 min.     Cooking: 3-5 min.     Serves: 1-2*

*Instructions:*

1. Preheat the air fryer to 180°C (350°F).
2. Place the bread slices in the air fryer basket and toast for 3-5 minutes, or until they reach desired crispness.
3. Spread a generous layer of cream cheese on the warm toast.
4. Arrange smoked salmon slices over the cream cheese.
5. Garnish with fresh dill or chives, and capers if desired.
6. Serve with a lemon wedge on the side for a fresh, zesty finish.

*Ingredients:*

1. 2 slices of whole-grain or rye bread
2. 4 ounces of smoked salmon
3. Cream cheese or a creamy cheese spread
4. Fresh dill or chives, finely chopped
5. Capers (optional)
6. Lemon wedges for serving
7. Salt and pepper to taste

*Calories: 300-500   Fat: 15-20g   Carbohydrates: 20-30g   Protein: 15-25g   Fiber: 2-4g*

# Toasts

## Banana Peanut Butter Toast

*Prep: 5 min.    Cooking: 3-5 min.    Serves: 1-2*

*Instructions:*
1. Preheat the air fryer to 180°C (350°F).
2. Place the bread slices in the air fryer basket and toast for 3-5 minutes, or until they are crispy and golden.
3. Spread peanut butter evenly on each slice of toasted bread.
4. Slice the banana and arrange the slices on top of the peanut butter.

*Ingredients:*
1. 2 slices of bread (whole grain is a good option)
2. 1 ripe banana
3. 2 tablespoons of peanut butter

*Calories: 300-350   Fat: 16-18g   Carbohydrates: 30-40g   Protein: 10-12g.   Fiber: 5-6g*

## Mushroom Garlic Toast

*Prep: 10 min.    Cooking: 8-10 min.    Serves: 1-2*

*Instructions:*
1. Preheat the air fryer to 180°C (350°F).
2. In a pan, heat the olive oil or butter and sauté the garlic and mushrooms until they are tender and golden, seasoning with salt and pepper.
3. Place the bread slices in the air fryer basket and toast for 3-5 minutes, or until crispy.
4. Top the toasted bread with the sautéed mushroom and garlic mixture.
5. Garnish with fresh herbs before serving.

*Ingredients:*
1. 2 2 slices of bread (such as sourdough or whole grain)
2. 1 cup of sliced mushrooms (button, cremini, or your choice)
3. 2 cloves of garlic, minced
4. 2 tablespoons of olive oil or butter
5. Salt and pepper to taste
6. Fresh herbs (like parsley or thyme) for garnish

*Calories: 250-300    Fat: 14-16g    Carbohydrates: 20-25g   Protein: 6-8g    Fiber: 3-4g*

# Toasts

## Berry Ricotta Toast

*Prep: 5 min.     Cooking: 3-5 min.     Serves: 1-2*

*Instructions:*
1. Preheat the air fryer to 180°C (350°F).
2. Place the bread slices in the air fryer basket and toast for 3-5 minutes, or until they are golden and crispy.
3. Spread the ricotta cheese evenly over each slice of toasted bread.
4. Top with a generous amount of mixed berries.
5. Drizzle with honey or maple syrup and garnish with mint leaves if desired.

*Ingredients:*
1. 2 slices of bread (whole grain or artisanal)
2. 1/2 cup ricotta cheese
3. 1/2 cup mixed berries (such as strawberries, blueberries, raspberries)
4. Honey or maple syrup for drizzling (optional)
5. Mint leaves for garnish (optional)

Calories: 200-250   Fat: 8-10g   Carbohydrates: 25-30g   Protein: 10-12g.   Fiber: 4-5g

## Ham and Cheese Toast

*Prep: 5 min.     Cooking: 5-7 min.     Serves: 1-2*

*Instructions:*
1. Preheat the air fryer to 180°C (350°F).
2. Lightly butter or spread mayonnaise on one side of each bread slice.
3. Place a slice of cheese on the unbuttered side of one bread slice, add the ham, then top with another slice of cheese, and cover with the second slice of bread, buttered side up.
4. Put the sandwich in the air fryer basket and cook for 5-7 minutes, flipping halfway through, or until the bread is golden brown and the cheese has melted.

*Ingredients:*
1. 2 slices of bread (such as white, whole grain, or sourdough)
2. 2 slices of ham
3. 2 slices of cheese (such as cheddar, Swiss, or your preferred type)
4. Butter or mayonnaise (for spreading on the bread)

Calories: 300-400   Fat: 16-22g   Carbohydrates: 20-30g   Protein: 15-25g   Fiber: 1-3g

# Toasts

## Almond Butter and Apple Toast

*Prep: 5 min.    Cooking: 3-5 min.    Serves: 1-2*

*Instructions:*
1. Preheat the air fryer to 180°C (350°F).
2. Toast the bread slices in the air fryer for 3-5 minutes, or until they reach your desired level of crispiness.
3. Spread a generous amount of almond butter on each slice of toasted bread.
4. Arrange the thin apple slices on top of the almond butter.
5. Optionally, sprinkle with cinnamon and drizzle with honey or maple syrup for added flavor.

*Ingredients:*
1. 2 slices of bread (whole grain or your choice)
2. Almond butter
3. 1 apple, thinly sliced
4. A sprinkle of cinnamon (optional)
5. Honey or maple syrup for drizzling (optional)

*Calories: 250-350   Fat: 14-18g   Carbohydrates: 30-40g   Protein: 8-10g.   Fiber: 5-7g*

## Chocolate Hazelnut Spread Toast

*Prep: 10 min.    Cooking: 5-7 min.    Serves: 1-2*

*Instructions:*
1. Preheat the air fryer to 180°C (350°F).
2. Brush the bread slices lightly with olive oil and place them in the air fryer basket.
3. Toast the bread in the air fryer for 3-4 minutes, or until golden and crispy.
4. Warm the prepared caponata in a pan if needed, then spoon it generously onto the toasted bread slices.
5. Garnish with fresh basil leaves and serve immediately.

*Ingredients:*
1. 2 slices of rustic bread (such as ciabatta or sourdough)
2. 1 cup prepared Sicilian caponata (eggplant, capers, olives, tomatoes, vinegar)
3. Olive oil (for brushing the bread)
4. Fresh basil leaves for garnish

*Calories: 200-300   Fat: 10-15g   Carbohydrates: 30-40g   Protein: 5-10g   Fiber: 5-7g*

# Toasts

## Avocado and Egg Toast

*Prep: 10 min.    Cooking: 10 min.    Serves: 2*

Instructions:

6. Preheat your air fryer to 350°F (175°C).
7. Slice the avocado in half and remove the pit. Scoop out a bit of flesh from each half to create a larger hollow for the egg.
8. Crack one egg into each avocado half. Season with salt and pepper to taste.
9. Place the avocado halves in the air fryer basket, cut side up. Make sure they are stable and won't tip over.
10. Air fry the avocado halves for about 8-10 minutes, or until the eggs are cooked to your desired level of doneness. If you prefer a runny yolk, aim for about 8 minutes; for a firmer yolk, cook for closer to 10 minutes.
11. While the avocado and eggs are cooking, toast the slices of whole grain bread until golden brown.
12. Once the eggs are cooked, carefully remove the avocado halves from the air fryer using tongs or a spatula.
13. Place each avocado half on top of a slice of toasted bread.
14. Serve immediately, garnished with optional toppings such as sliced cherry tomatoes, chopped fresh herbs, or a drizzle of hot sauce.

Ingredients:
1. 1 ripe avocado
2. 2 large eggs
3. 2 slices of whole grain bread
4. Salt and pepper to taste
5. Optional toppings: sliced cherry tomatoes, chopped fresh herbs (such as parsley or chives), hot sauce

*Calories: 320   Fat: 18g   Carbohydrates: 27g   Protein: 15g.   Fiber: 10g*

## Tuna Salad Toast

*Prep: 10 min.    Cooking: 3-5 min.    Serves: 1-2*

Instructions:

1. In a bowl, mix the drained tuna with mayonnaise or Greek yogurt, celery, red onion, salt, and pepper to make the tuna salad.
2. Preheat the air fryer to 180°C (350°F).
3. Toast the bread slices in the air fryer for 3-5 minutes, or until golden brown and crispy.
4. Spread the tuna salad evenly on the toasted bread slices.
5. If desired, top the tuna salad with lettuce, tomato, or cucumber slices.

Ingredients:
1. 2 slices of bread (whole grain or your choice)
2. 1 can of tuna, drained
3. 2 tablespoons of mayonnaise or Greek yogurt
4. 1 tablespoon of chopped celery
5. 1 tablespoon of chopped red onion
6. Salt and pepper to taste
7. Optional: lettuce leaves, sliced tomato, or cucumber for topping

*Calories: 250-350   Fat: 10-15g   Carbohydrates: 20-30g   Protein: 20-25g   Fiber: 2-4g*

# Toasts

## Maple Cinnamon Toast

*Prep: 5 min.    Cooking: 3-5 min.    Serves: 1-2*

*Instructions:*
1. Preheat the air fryer to 180°C (350°F).
2. Spread butter on one side of each bread slice.
3. Mix the maple syrup and cinnamon in a small bowl, then brush or drizzle the mixture over the buttered side of each bread slice.
4. Place the bread, maple-cinnamon side up, in the air fryer basket and cook for 3-5 minutes, or until the bread is toasted and the topping is slightly caramelized.
5. Optionally, sprinkle with powdered sugar or drizzle with a bit more maple syrup and a dash of vanilla extract before serving.

*Ingredients:*
1. 2 slices of bread (preferably thick-cut for best results)
2. Butter or a butter alternative, softened
3. 2 tablespoons of maple syrup
4. 1 teaspoon of ground cinnamon
5. Optional: a sprinkle of powdered sugar or a dash of vanilla extract for extra flavor

*Calories: 200-300   Fat: 6-10g    Carbohydrates: 40-50g   Protein: 3-5g.   Fiber: 1-2g*

# Porridge

## Muesli

*Prep: 10 min.    Cooking: 10-15 min.    Serves: 4*

*Instructions:*
8. Preheat the air fryer to 160°C (320°F).
9. In a bowl, mix the oats, nuts, and seeds.
10. Spread the mixture evenly in the air fryer basket.
11. Toast in the air fryer for 10-15 minutes, stirring occasionally, until the mixture is golden and fragrant.
12. Let the toasted mixture cool, then transfer it to a bowl mix with dried fruits and cinnamon.
13. Serve the muesli in bowls, topped with Greek yogurt a drizzle of honey.

*Ingredients:*
1. 1 cup rolled oats
2. 1/2 cup mixed nuts (such as almonds, walnuts, and pistachios), chopped
3. 1/4 cup seeds (such as pumpkin or sunflower seeds)
4. 1/2 cup mixed dried    and fruits (such as apricots, figs, and raisins),    and chopped
5. 1 teaspoon ground cinnamon
6. Greek yogurt, for serving
7. Honey, for drizzling

*Calories: 300-400   Fat: 10-15g    Carbohydrates: 45-50g   Protein: 10-15g.   Fiber: 6-8g*

# Porridge

## Millet and Apricot Porridge

*Prep: 10min.      Cooking: 20-25min.      Serves: 4*

| Ingredients: |
| --- |

*Instructions:*

1. Preheat the air fryer to 160°C (320°F).
2. In an air fryer-safe dish, combine the millet, almond milk, dried apricots, cardamom, and nutmeg.
3. Cover the dish with foil or a suitable lid and place it in the air fryer basket.
4. Cook for 20-25 minutes, stirring occasionally, until the millet is tender and has absorbed most of the milk.
5. Stir the porridge well and let it sit for a few minutes to thicken. Sweeten with honey or maple syrup if desired.
6. Serve warm, perhaps with a sprinkle of extra chopped apricots or a dash of milk.

Ingredients:
1. 1 cup millet, rinsed
2. 3 cups almond milk (or other plant-based milk)
3. 1/2 cup dried apricots, chopped
4. 1/2 teaspoon ground cardamom
5. 1/4 teaspoon ground nutmeg
6. Honey or maple syrup to taste (optional)

*Calories: 250-300   Fat: 3-5g   Carbohydrates: 50-60g  Protein: 6-10g.   Fiber: 5-7g*

## Barley Porridge

*Prep: 5 min.   Cooking: 30-35 min.    Serves: 4*

*Instructions:*

7. Pre-soak the barley overnight in water if you want to reduce cooking time and enhance digestibility. Drain and rinse before cooking.
8. Preheat the air fryer to 160°C (320°F).
9. In a heat-resistant air fryer-safe dish, mix the barley, almond milk, dates or honey, orange zest, cinnamon, and a pinch of salt.
10. Place the dish in the air fryer basket and cook for 30-35 minutes, stirring occasionally, until the barley is tender and the mixture has thickened to a porridge consistency. Add more almond milk during cooking if needed for desired texture.
11. Serve warm, with additional toppings like nuts, fresh fruit, or a sprinkle of cinnamon if desired.

Ingredients:
1. 1 cup pearl barley, rinsed
2. 4 cups almond milk (or more for desired consistency)
3. 1/4 cup dates, pitted and chopped, or honey to taste
4. 1 teaspoon orange zest
5. 1/2 teaspoon ground cinnamon
6. Pinch of salt

*Calories: 200-250   Fat: 2-3g   Carbohydrates: 40-50g   Protein: 5-10g.   Fiber: 9-10g*

# Porridge

## Greek Honey and Nut Cornflakes

*Prep: 5 min.    Cooking: 3-5 min.    Serves: 1*

*Instructions:*
1. Preheat the air fryer to 180°C (350°F).
2. Place the walnuts in the air fryer basket and toast for 3-5 minutes or until they are lightly browned and fragrant. Be careful to avoid burning.
3. In a bowl, layer the cornflakes with Greek yogurt.
4. Drizzle honey over the yogurt and sprinkle with toasted walnuts.
5. Top with fresh berries and serve immediately.

*Ingredients:*
1. 1 cup cornflakes
2. 1/2 cup Greek yogurt
3. 2 tablespoons honey
4. 1/4 cup walnuts
5. 1/2 cup fresh berries (like strawberries, blueberries, or raspberries)

*Calories: 300-350   Fat: 10-15g   Carbohydrates: 45-50g   Protein: 10-15g.   Fiber: 3-5g*

## Bulgur Wheat Breakfast Bowl

*Prep: 5 min.    Cooking: 25-25 min.    Serves: 2-3*

*Instructions:*
8. Preheat the air fryer to 180°C (350°F).
9. Rinse the bulgur wheat and place it in an air fryer-safe dish. Add a pinch of salt and optional cinnamon or vanilla, then pour in the milk or water.
10. Cook in the air fryer for 20-25 minutes, stirring occasionally, until the bulgur is tender and has absorbed the liquid.
11. While the bulgur is cooking, toast the chopped nuts in the air fryer for 3-5 minutes until golden brown and fragrant. Set aside.
12. Once the bulgur is cooked, fluff it with a fork and let it cool slightly.
13. Stir in the dried fruits and toasted nuts, then sweeten with brown sugar or drizzle with honey to taste.
14. Serve warm, with extra milk if desired.

*Ingredients:*
1. 1 cup bulgur wheat
2. 2 cups milk (dairy or plant-based) or water for cooking
3. 1/4 cup mixed nuts (such as almonds, walnuts, and pecans), chopped
4. 1/4 cup dried fruits (like raisins, apricots, or cranberries), chopped
5. 1-2 tablespoons brown sugar or honey
6. Pinch of salt
7. Optional: cinnamon or vanilla extract for added flavor

*Calories: 300-400   Fat: 10-15g   Carbohydrates: 50-60g Protein: 10-15g.   Fiber: 8-10g*

# Porridge

## Savory Oatmeal with Feta and Olives

*Prep: 5 min.     Cooking: 15-20 min.     Serves: 2*

*Instructions:*

1. Preheat the air fryer to 180°C (350°F).
2. In an air fryer-safe dish, combine the oats and vegetable broth. Season with a little salt and pepper.
3. Place the dish in the air fryer and cook for 15-20 minutes, stirring occasionally, until the oatmeal is creamy and has absorbed most of the broth.
4. Remove from the air fryer and stir in the crumbled feta cheese and chopped olives. Let it sit for a minute to allow the feta to slightly melt into the warm oatmeal.
5. Garnish with fresh herbs before serving.

*Ingredients:*
1. 1 cup rolled oats
2. 2 cups vegetable broth
3. 1/2 cup crumbled feta cheese
4. 1/4 cup chopped olives (green or black)
5. Fresh herbs (such as parsley or thyme), finely chopped
6. Salt and pepper to taste

*Calories: 250-300   Fat: 10-15g   Carbohydrates: 30-35g  Protein: 10-15g.   Fiber: 4-6g*

## Couscous Breakfast Pudding

*Prep: 5 min.     Cooking: 15-20 min.     Serves: 2-3*

*Instructions:*

7. Preheat the air fryer to 160°C (320°F).
8. In an air fryer-safe dish, combine the couscous, milk (or milk alternative), honey (or maple syrup), cinnamon, and nutmeg. Stir well to mix.
9. Cover the dish with aluminum foil or an appropriate lid and place it in the air fryer basket.
10. Cook for 15-20 minutes, stirring halfway through, until the couscous is tender and has absorbed the liquid, achieving a pudding-like consistency.
11. Remove from the air fryer and let it sit for a few minutes to thicken further.
12. Serve warm, topped with your choice of fresh fruits, nuts, or dried fruits.

*Ingredients:*
1. 1 cup couscous
2. 2 cups milk or milk alternative (e.g., almond, coconut, or oat milk)
3. 2-3 tablespoons honey or maple syrup
4. 1/2 teaspoon ground cinnamon
5. 1/4 teaspoon ground nutmeg
6. Optional toppings: fresh fruits, nuts, or dried fruits

*Calories: 300-350   Fat: 2-5g   Carbohydrates: 60-70g   Protein: 10-15g.   Fiber: 3-5g*

# Porridge

## Farro with Roasted Vegetables

*Prep: 10min.     Cooking: 30 minutes for farro,  15-20 minutes for vegetables.*
*Serves: 2-3*

*Instructions:*

1. Preheat the air fryer to 200°C (390°F).
2. Cook farro in water or vegetable broth according to package instructions until tender, usually about 25-30 minutes. Drain any excess liquid and set aside.
3. While the farro is cooking, toss the sliced vegetables with 1 tablespoon of olive oil, salt, and pepper.
4. Spread the vegetables in the air fryer basket and roast for 15-20 minutes, shaking the basket halfway through, until they are tender and charred at the edges.
5. In a large bowl, combine the cooked farro with the roasted vegetables. Drizzle with the remaining olive oil and balsamic vinegar, and toss to coat evenly.
6. Season with salt and pepper to taste and garnish with fresh herbs before serving.

| Ingredients: |
| --- |
| 1. 1 cup farro, rinsed and drained |
| 2. 2 cups water or vegetable broth (for cooking farro) |
| 3. 1 bell pepper, sliced |
| 4. 1 zucchini, sliced |
| 5. 1 small eggplant, sliced |
| 6. 2 tablespoons olive oil, divided |
| 7. 1 tablespoon balsamic vinegar |
| 8. Salt and pepper to taste |
| 9. Fresh herbs (such as basil or parsley) for garnish |

*Calories: 300-400   Fat: 10-15g   Carbohydrates: 50-60g  Protein: 10-15g.   Fiber: 10-15g*

## Quinoa Fruit Salad

*Prep: 10 min.     Cooking: 15-20 min.     Serves: 4*

Instructions:

9. Cook quinoa in water according to package instructions, usually about 15-20 minutes, until all water is absorbed and quinoa is tender. Let it cool to room temperature.
10. In a large bowl, combine the cooled quinoa with diced fresh fruits, toasted nuts, and chopped mint leaves.
11. In a small bowl, whisk together lemon juice, honey, and a pinch of salt to create the dressing.
12. Pour the dressing over the quinoa and fruit mixture and toss gently to combine everything evenly.
13. Chill in the refrigerator for at least 30 minutes before serving to allow flavors to meld.

| Ingredients: |
| --- |
| 1. 1 cup quinoa, rinsed |
| 2. 2 cups water (for cooking quinoa) |
| 3. 1 cup diced fresh fruits (such as apples, berries, and oranges) |
| 4. 1/4 cup nuts (such as almonds or walnuts), toasted |
| 5. Mint leaves, finely chopped |
| 6. 2 tablespoons lemon juice |
| 7. 1 tablespoon honey |
| 8. Pinch of salt |

*Calories: 200-250   Fat: 5-10g   Carbohydrates: 35-40g   Protein: 6-8g.   Fiber: 5-7g*

# Porridge

## Polenta with Mushroom and Tomato Ragout

*Prep: 10min.    Cooking: 20 minutes for polenta, 15-20 minutes for ragout.    Serves: 4*

Instructions:
1. Cook the polenta according to package instructions, typically by boiling water or broth, adding the polenta gradually, and stirring constantly to prevent lumps. Cook until thick and creamy, then stir in butter or olive oil, and season with salt.
2. For the Mushroom and Tomato Ragout:

3. Preheat the air fryer to 200°C (390°F).
4. In a bowl, toss the mushrooms, cherry tomatoes, onion, and garlic with olive oil, salt, and pepper.
5. Spread the mixture in the air fryer basket and cook for 15-20 minutes, shaking occasionally, until vegetables are tender and lightly browned.
6. Mix in fresh herbs towards the end of cooking.
7. To serve, spoon the creamy polenta into bowls and top with the mushroom and tomato ragout.

*Calories: 300-350   Fat: 10-15g    Carbohydrates: 45-50g*
*Protein: 8-10g.    Fiber: 5-7g*

Ingredients:
1. 1 cup polenta (cornmeal)
2. 4 cups water or vegetable broth
3. Salt to taste
4. 2 tablespoons butter or olive oil
5. Ingredients for Ragout:
6.
7. 2 cups mushrooms, sliced
8. 1 cup cherry tomatoes, halved
9. 1 onion, finely chopped
10. 2 cloves garlic, minced
11. 2 tablespoons olive oil
12. Salt and pepper to taste
13. Fresh herbs (like thyme or basil), chopped

## Semolina Porridge with Citrus and Dates

*Prep: 5min.      Cooking: 20-25min.      Serves: 4*

*Instructions:*
1. In a large, air fryer-safe dish, mix the semolina and milk. Stir in the orange zest and sweetener if using.
2. Preheat the air fryer to 160°C (320°F).
3. Place the dish in the air fryer and cook for 20-25 minutes, stirring occasionally, until the semolina is cooked through and the porridge has thickened to your desired consistency.
4. Remove from the air fryer and let it cool slightly. Stir in the chopped dates and sprinkle with cinnamon before serving.

Ingredients:
1. 1 cup semolina
2. 4 cups milk (dairy or plant-based)
3. Zest of 1 orange
4. 1/2 cup chopped dates
5. 1 teaspoon ground cinnamon
6. 2 tablespoons honey or sugar (optional for sweetness)

*Calories: 250-300   Fat: 2-5g   Carbohydrates: 50-55g   Protein: 8-10g.    Fiber: 3-4g*

# Porridge

## Spelt Pancakes with Fig Compote

*Prep: 15 min.    Cooking: 15-20 min.    Serves: 2-3*

*Instructions:*
*For the Fig Compote:*
1. In a small saucepan, combine the chopped figs, lemon zest, honey, and water. Simmer over low heat until the figs are soft and the mixture has thickened into a compote, about 10-15 minutes. Set aside.

*For the Pancakes:*
2. In a bowl, mix spelt flour, sugar (if using), baking powder, and salt.
3. In another bowl, whisk together milk, egg, and melted butter or oil.
4. Combine the wet and dry ingredients, stirring until just mixed (the batter should be slightly lumpy).
5. Preheat the air fryer to 180°C (350°F) and place parchment paper in the air fryer basket.
6. Spoon the batter onto the parchment paper in the air fryer, forming small pancakes.
7. Cook for 4-6 minutes or until the pancakes are golden brown and cooked through, flipping halfway.
8. Serve the spelt pancakes with the warm fig compote on top.

*Ingredients:*
1. 1 cup spelt flour
2. 1 tablespoon sugar (optional)
3. 1 teaspoon baking powder
4. 1/2 teaspoon salt
5. 1 cup milk (dairy or plant-based)
6. 1 egg
7. 1 tablespoon melted butter or oil
8. Ingredients for Fig Compote:
9. 
10. 1 cup fresh or dried figs, chopped
11. Zest of 1 lemon
12. 2 tablespoons honey
13. 1/4 cup water

*Calories: 300-400   Fat: 8-12g   Carbohydrates: 50-60g   Protein: 10-15g.   Fiber: 8-10g*


## Rye Bread French Toast

*Prep: 10 min.    Cooking: 8-10 min.    Serves: 2-4*

*Instructions:*
1. In a bowl, whisk together the eggs, milk, cinnamon, and vanilla extract until well combined.
2. Dip each slice of rye bread into the egg mixture, ensuring both sides are well coated.
3. Preheat the air fryer to 180°C (350°F) and lightly grease the air fryer basket with butter or oil.
4. Place the soaked bread slices in the air fryer basket, making sure they do not overlap.
5. Cook for 4-5 minutes on each side, or until the French toast is golden brown and cooked through.
6. Serve the French toast warm, topped with Greek yogurt and fruit compote.

*Ingredients:*
1. 4 slices of rye bread
2. 2 eggs
3. 1/2 cup milk (dairy or plant-based)
4. 1 teaspoon ground cinnamon
5. 1 teaspoon vanilla extract (optional)
6. Butter or oil for greasing
7. Greek yogurt and fruit compote for serving

*Calories: 200-300   Fat: 8-12g   Carbohydrates: 30-40g   Protein: 10-15g.   Fiber: 4-6g*

# Pancake

## Greek Yogurt Pancakes

*Prep: 10 min.    Cooking: 15 min.    Serves: 2-3*

*Instructions:*

1. In a large bowl, mix together the flour, baking powder, baking soda, and salt.
2. In another bowl, combine the Greek yogurt, honey, egg, and vanilla extract until smooth.
3. Fold the wet ingredients into the dry ingredients until just combined, careful not to overmix.
4. Preheat the air fryer to 180°C (350°F) and lightly grease the air fryer basket.
5. Spoon the batter into the air fryer in batches, forming small pancakes. Cook for 7-8 minutes, flipping halfway through, until the pancakes are golden brown and cooked through.
6. Serve the pancakes warm, topped with additional honey and chopped walnuts.

*Ingredients:*
1. 1 cup all-purpose flour
2. 1 teaspoon baking powder
3. 1/2 teaspoon baking soda
4. 1/4 teaspoon salt
5. 1 cup Greek yogurt
6. 1-2 tablespoons honey, plus more for serving
7. 1 egg
8. 1/2 teaspoon vanilla extract (optional)
9. Chopped walnuts for topping

*Calories: 200-350   Fat: 5-10g   Carbohydrates: 45-50g   Protein: 10-20g.   Fiber: 1-2g*

## Socca (Chickpea Flour Pancakes)

*Prep: 10min. (plus 30 minutes resting time for the batter)    Cooking: 8-10min.    Serves: 2-4*

*Instructions:*

1. In a bowl, whisk together chickpea flour, water, olive oil, salt, and chopped herbs until smooth. Let the batter rest for 30 minutes to allow the flour to absorb the water.
2. Preheat the air fryer to 200°C (390°F). Grease the air fryer basket with a little olive oil.
3. Pour the batter into the basket, forming a thin layer (cook in batches if necessary).
4. Cook for 4-5 minutes, then flip carefully and cook for another 4-5 minutes, or until the socca is firm and the edges are starting to crisp.
5. Remove from the air fryer, sprinkle with freshly ground black pepper, and slice into wedges or squares.
6. Serve warm, either plain or with toppings like sautéed vegetables or a dollop of pesto.

*Ingredients:*
1. 1 cup chickpea flour (gram flour)
2. 1 1/4 cups water
3. 2 tablespoons olive oil, plus extra for greasing
4. 1/2 teaspoon salt
5. Fresh herbs (such as rosemary, thyme, or parsley), finely chopped
6. Freshly ground black pepper

*Calories: 150-200   Fat: 7-10g   Carbohydrates: 15-20g   Protein: 5-7g.   Fiber: 2-3g*

# Pancake

## Italian Ricotta Pancakes

*Prep: 15 min.    Cooking: 15-20 min.    Serves: 2-4*

Instructions:
1. In a bowl, combine flour, baking powder, salt, and sugar.
2. In another bowl, mix ricotta cheese, milk, egg yolks, lemon zest, and vanilla extract until smooth.
3. Gradually add the dry ingredients to the wet ingredients, stirring until just combined.
4. In a separate bowl, beat the egg whites until stiff peaks form, then gently fold into the batter.
5. Preheat the air fryer to 180°C (350°F) and grease the basket with butter or oil.
6. Spoon the batter into the air fryer, forming small pancakes, and cook for about 7-10 minutes, flipping halfway through, until golden brown and cooked through.
7. For the syrup, warm the maple syrup or honey with the lemon zest in a small pot over low heat or in the microwave.
8. Serve the pancakes hot, drizzled with the lemon zest-infused syrup.

Ingredients:
1. 1 cup all-purpose flour
2. 2 teaspoons baking powder
3. 1/4 teaspoon salt
4. 2 tablespoons sugar
5. 3/4 cup ricotta cheese
6. 1/2 cup milk
7. 2 eggs, separated
8. Zest of 1 lemon
9. 1 teaspoon vanilla extract
10. Butter or oil for greasing
11. For the Lemon Zest-Infused

*Syrup:*
12.
13. 1/2 cup maple syrup or honey
14. Zest of 1 lemon

*Calories: 300-400   Fat: 10-15g   Carbohydrates: 40-50g   Protein: 10-20g.   Fiber: 1-2g*

## Egyptian Fava Bean Pancakes (Ta'amia)

*Prep: 15min.    Cooking: 10-15min.    Serves: 4*

Instructions:
1. In a large bowl, combine mashed fava beans, parsley, onion, garlic, cumin, coriander, salt, and pepper. If the mixture needs binding, add an egg.
2. Mix well until all ingredients are evenly distributed and the mixture can be formed into patties.
3. Preheat the air fryer to 200°C (390°F) and lightly grease the basket with olive oil.
4. Form the mixture into small pancake-sized patties and place them in the air fryer basket, ensuring they don't overlap.
5. Cook for 5-7 minutes on each side or until golden brown and crispy.
6. Serve the fava bean pancakes warm with tahini sauce on the side.

Ingredients:
1. 2 cups cooked fava beans, mashed
2. 1/2 cup fresh parsley, finely chopped
3. 1 small onion, finely chopped
4. 2 garlic cloves, minced
5. 1 teaspoon ground cumin
6. 1/2 teaspoon ground coriander
7. Salt and pepper to taste
8. 1 egg (optional, to bind the mixture)
9. Olive oil for greasing
10. Tahini sauce for serving

*Calories: 250-300   Fat: 5-10g   Carbohydrates: 40-45g   Protein: 12-20g.   Fiber: 8-10g*

# Pancake

## Spanish Churro Pancakes

*Prep: 10min.    Cooking: 15-20min.    Serves: 2-4*

*Instructions:*

1. In a large bowl, mix together flour, baking powder, salt, and sugar. In another bowl, whisk together milk, egg, and vanilla extract.
2. Combine the wet and dry ingredients, stirring until smooth.
3. Preheat the air fryer to 180°C (350°F) and lightly grease the basket.
4. Pour batter into the air fryer in batches, forming small pancakes, and cook for about 7-10 minutes, flipping halfway through, until golden brown and cooked through.
5. Mix the sugar and cinnamon in a shallow dish. While pancakes are still warm, coat them in the cinnamon-sugar mixture.
6. For the chocolate sauce, heat the chocolate and cream in a small saucepan over low heat (or in the microwave), stirring until smooth and combined.
7. Serve the pancakes warm, drizzled with the chocolate sauce.

*Ingredients:*
*Ingredients for Pancakes:*
1. 1 cup all-purpose flour
2. 2 teaspoons baking powder
3. 1/4 teaspoon salt
4. 2 tablespoons sugar
5. 1 cup milk
6. 1 egg
7. 1 teaspoon vanilla extract
8. Butter or oil for greasing

*For the Cinnamon-Sugar Coating:*
9. 1/4 cup sugar
10. 1 tablespoon ground cinnamon

*For the Chocolate Sauce:*
11. 1/2 cup chocolate chips or chopped chocolate
12. 1/4 cup heavy cream or milk

## Moroccan Semolina Pancakes (Baghrir)

*Prep: 10 minutes (plus resting time for the batter to rise, about 30-60 minutes).*
*Cooking: 15-20 min.    Serves: 4-6*

*Instructions:*

1. In a blender, combine the semolina flour, all-purpose flour, instant yeast, baking powder, salt, and warm water. Blend until the batter is smooth and lump-free.
2. Let the batter rest in a warm place for 30-60 minutes, or until it becomes bubbly and has risen.
3. Preheat the air fryer to 180°C (350°F).
4. Pour small amounts of batter into the air fryer basket to form pancakes. Due to the unique texture of Baghrir, they are only cooked on one side, so there's no need to flip. Cook for 4-5 minutes or until the surface is full of bubbles and the edges are set.
5. Remove the Baghrir carefully and repeat with the remaining batter.
6. Serve the pancakes warm, topped with a generous drizzle of honey and melted butter.

*Ingredients:*
1. 1 cup fine semolina flour
2. 1/2 cup all-purpose flour
3. 1 teaspoon instant yeast
4. 1 teaspoon baking powder
5. 1/2 teaspoon salt
6. 2 cups warm water
7. Honey and melted butter for serving

*Calories: 200-250    Fat: 2-5g    Carbohydrates: 40-50g    Protein: 6-8g.    Fiber: 2-4g*

*Calories: 350-450    Fat: 15-20g    Carbohydrates: 50-60g    Protein: 8-10g.    Fiber: 2-3g*

# Pancake

## Cypriot Halloumi Pancakes

*Prep: 10 min.       Cooking: 10-15 min.       Serves: 2-4*

*Instructions:*

1. In a mixing bowl, combine the flour and baking powder.
2. Stir in the grated halloumi and chopped mint.
3. In a separate bowl, whisk together the milk and egg, then add to the dry ingredients, mixing until just combined into a batter.
4. Preheat the air fryer to 180°C (350°F) and lightly grease the basket with olive oil or butter.
5. Spoon the batter into the air fryer, forming small pancakes, and cook for 5-7 minutes on each side, or until they are golden brown and cooked through.
6. Serve the pancakes warm, ideally with a side of Greek yogurt or a light, refreshing cucumber salad.

*Ingredients:*
1. 1 cup all-purpose flour
2. 1 teaspoon baking powder
3. 1/2 cup grated halloumi cheese
4. 1 tablespoon fresh mint, finely chopped
5. 1 cup milk
6. 1 egg
7. Olive oil or butter for greasing

*Calories: 300-350   Fat: 15-20g   Carbohydrates: 30-35g   Protein: 15-35g.   Fiber: 1-2g*

## Israeli Cottage Cheese Pancakes

*Prep: 10 min.       Cooking: 10-15 min.       Serves: 2-4*

*Instructions:*

1. In a mixing bowl, combine the cottage cheese, flour, eggs, sugar, vanilla extract, and a pinch of salt. Stir until the batter is smooth.
2. Preheat the air fryer to 180°C (350°F) and lightly grease the basket with butter or oil.
3. Spoon the batter into the air fryer, forming small pancakes, and cook for about 5-7 minutes on each side, or until they are golden brown and set.
4. Serve the pancakes warm, topped with fresh fruit and a generous drizzle of silan (date syrup).

*Ingredients:*
1. 1 cup cottage cheese
2. 1/2 cup all-purpose flour
3. 2 eggs
4. 1 tablespoon sugar
5. 1 teaspoon vanilla extract
6. Pinch of salt
7. Fresh fruit (such as berries, sliced bananas, or figs) for serving
8. Silan (date syrup) for drizzling
9. Butter or oil for greasing

*Calories: 200-300   Fat: 6-10g   Carbohydrates: 30-40g   Protein: 6-10g.   Fiber: 1-3g*

# Pancake

## Egyptian Fava Bean Pancakes (Ta'amia)

*Prep: 10min. (plus time for saffron to infuse)     Cooking: 10-15min.     Serves: 2-4*

*Instructions:*

1. In a small bowl, dissolve the saffron threads in warm water and let it steep for a few minutes to release its color and flavor.
2. In a large mixing bowl, whisk together the flour, baking powder, salt, and sugar.
3. In another bowl, beat together the milk, egg, and saffron infusion.
4. Combine the wet and dry ingredients, stirring until the batter is smooth.
5. Preheat the air fryer to 180°C (350°F) and lightly grease the basket with butter or oil.
6. Spoon the batter into the air fryer, forming small pancakes, and cook for about 5-7 minutes on each side, or until golden brown and cooked through.
7. Serve the pancakes warm, drizzled with additional honey or sprinkled with sugar, if desired.

*Ingredients:*

1. 1 cup all-purpose flour
2. 2 teaspoons baking powder
3. 1/4 teaspoon salt
4. 2 tablespoons sugar or honey
5. 1 cup milk
6. 1 egg
7. A pinch of saffron threads, dissolved in 1 tablespoon warm water
8. Butter or oil for greasing

*Calories: 200-300   Fat: 5-10g   Carbohydrates: 35-45g  Protein: 5-10g.   Fiber: 1-2g*

## Lebanese Potato Pancakes (Kibbet Batata)

*Prep: 20 min.     Cooking: 15-20 min.     Serves: 4*

*Instructions:*

1. Mash the boiled potatoes until smooth. Mix in the chopped onions, minced garlic, ground cumin, fresh herbs, salt, and pepper. If the mixture needs binding, add an egg.
2. Form the potato mixture into small patties.
3. Preheat the air fryer to 200°C (390°F) and lightly brush the air fryer basket with olive oil.
4. Place the potato patties in the basket, ensuring they don't overlap, and brush the tops with a little more olive oil.
5. Cook for 15-20 minutes, flipping halfway through, until the pancakes are golden brown and crispy.
6. Serve the potato pancakes warm with a side of labneh.

*Ingredients:*

8. 2 large potatoes, peeled and boiled
9. 1 onion, finely chopped
10. 2 garlic cloves, minced
11. 1 teaspoon ground cumin
12. 1/4 cup fresh herbs (such as parsley or cilantro), chopped
13. Salt and pepper to taste
14. 1 egg (optional, for binding)
15. Olive oil for brushing
16. Labneh for serving

*Calories: 200-250   Fat: 6-10g   Carbohydrates: 30-35g   Protein: 6-8g.   Fiber: 3-5g*

# Pancake

## Cretan Honey and Cheese Pancakes

*Prep: 10min.     Cooking: 15-20min.     Serves: 4*

*Instructions:*
1. In a bowl, whisk together the flour, baking powder, salt, and sugar.
2. In another bowl, beat the milk and egg, then combine with the dry ingredients to form a smooth batter.
3. Stir in the mizithra or ricotta cheese, gently folding it into the batter to keep the pancakes fluffy.
4. Preheat the air fryer to 180°C (350°F) and grease the basket with olive oil or butter.
5. Spoon the batter into the air fryer, forming small pancakes, and cook for about 7-10 minutes, flipping halfway through, until golden brown and cooked through.
6. Serve the pancakes warm, drizzled with thyme honey and sprinkled with chopped nuts.

*Ingredients:*
1. 1 cup all-purpose flour
2. 2 teaspoons baking powder
3. 1/4 teaspoon salt
4. 2 tablespoons sugar
5. 1 cup milk
6. 1 egg
7. 1/2 cup Cretan mizithra or ricotta cheese
8. Thyme honey for drizzling
9. Chopped nuts (walnuts, almonds, or hazelnuts) for topping
10. Olive oil or butter for greasing

*Calories: 300-350   Fat: 10-15g    Carbohydrates: 40-50g  Protein: 10-15g.   Fiber: 1-2g*

## Turkish Zucchini Pancakes (Mücver)

*Prep: 15min.     Cooking: 15-20min.     Serves: 4*

*Instructions:*
12. After grating the zucchini, place it in a colander, sprinkle with salt, and let it sit to draw out moisture. Squeeze the excess water from the zucchini.
13. In a bowl, mix the drained zucchini with crumbled feta cheese, chopped dill, flour, and eggs. Season with salt and pepper to create a thick batter.
14. Preheat the air fryer to 200°C (390°F) and lightly grease the basket with olive oil.
15. Spoon the zucchini batter into the air fryer, flattening into pancake shapes, and cook for about 7-10 minutes on each side until golden brown and crispy.
16. For the yogurt dip, combine Greek yogurt, minced garlic, chopped dill, salt, and lemon juice in a bowl and mix well.
17. Serve the zucchini pancakes warm with the yogurt dip on the side.

*Ingredients:*
1. 2 medium zucchinis, grated and drained
2. 1/2 cup feta cheese, crumbled
3. 2 tablespoons fresh dill, chopped
4. 1/2 cup all-purpose flour
5. 2 eggs
6. Salt and pepper to taste
7. Olive oil for greasing

*For the Yogurt Dip:*
8. 1 cup Greek yogurt
9. 1 clove garlic, minced
10. 1 tablespoon fresh dill, chopped
11. Salt and lemon juice to taste

*Calories: 250-300   Fat: 15-20g    Carbohydrates: 20-25g  Protein: 12-15g.   Fiber: 2-3g*

# Bonus Quick & Easy

Quick & Easy Mediterranean Air Grill Recipes

Elevate your culinary skills with our collection of quick and easy Mediterranean-inspired recipes designed specifically for the air grill. Perfect for busy weekdays or impromptu gatherings, these dishes boast all the vibrant flavors of the Mediterranean in minimal time. Get ready to impress your taste buds and guests alike with these delicious creations.

Kickstart your Mediterranean culinary adventure with a mouthwatering appetizer of grilled halloumi cheese. Simply slice the halloumi into thick pieces, brush with olive oil, and grill until golden brown and slightly crispy on the outside while remaining deliciously gooey on the inside. Serve with a side of fresh lemon wedges and a sprinkle of za'atar for an extra burst of flavor.

For a satisfying main course, try our speedy grilled shrimp skewers marinated in a tangy blend of lemon juice, garlic, and herbs. Thread succulent shrimp onto skewers and grill until pink and charred, infusing each bite with a delightful smokiness. Pair with a vibrant Mediterranean salsa made from diced tomatoes, cucumbers, red onions, and a drizzle of balsamic glaze for a refreshing finish.

Short on time but craving something hearty? Whip up a batch of grilled Mediterranean vegetable wraps filled with roasted peppers, eggplant, and zucchini. Grill the vegetables until tender and slightly charred, then wrap them in warm pita bread with a dollop of creamy hummus and a sprinkle of crumbled feta cheese. It's a satisfying meal that's bursting with flavor and ready in minutes.

For a lighter option, try our grilled Greek chicken salad tossed with crisp lettuce, juicy cherry tomatoes, cucumbers, and kalamata olives. Marinate chicken breast in a blend of olive oil, lemon juice, garlic, and oregano before grilling to juicy perfection. Slice the chicken and serve atop the salad with a drizzle of tzatziki sauce for a refreshing and nutritious meal that's ready to enjoy in no time.

Round out your Mediterranean feast with a quick and easy dessert like grilled fruit skewers. Thread chunks of pineapple, peaches, and strawberries onto skewers and grill until caramelized and fragrant. Serve with a scoop of creamy Greek yogurt and a sprinkle of honey for a light and refreshing end to your meal.

With these quick and easy Mediterranean air grill recipes, you can enjoy the bold flavors and healthful ingredients of the Mediterranean in no time at all.

# Quick & Easy

## Greek Chicken Thighs

*Prep: 10 minutes (plus at least 30 minutes for marinating)*       *Cooking: 25-25 min.*      *Serves: 4*

Instructions:
1. In a bowl, combine lemon juice and zest, olive oil, minced garlic, oregano, salt, and pepper to create the marinade.
2. Coat the chicken thighs in the marinade and let rest for at least 30 minutes in the refrigerator, or overnight for deeper flavor.
3. Preheat the air fryer to 180°C (350°F).
4. Place the marinated chicken thighs in the air fryer basket, skin side down, and cook for 10 minutes.
5. Flip the thighs and continue cooking for another 10-15 minutes, or until the chicken is cooked through and the skin is crispy.
6. Let the chicken rest for a few minutes before serving to retain its juices.

Ingredients:
1. 4 chicken thighs, bone-in, skin-on
2. Juice and zest of 1 lemon
3. 2 tablespoons olive oil
4. 3 cloves garlic, minced
5. 1 tablespoon dried oregano
6. Salt and pepper to taste

*Calories: 300   Fat: 22g   Carbohydrates: 1g   Protein: 24g.   Fiber: 0g*

## Falafel

*Prep: 15min.    Cooking: 10-15min.    Serves: 4*

Instructions:
1. In a food processor, combine chickpeas, onion, garlic, parsley, cilantro, cumin, coriander, salt, pepper, and cayenne. Pulse until mixture is coarsely ground.
2. Add flour and baking powder to the mixture and pulse until it's well combined and holds together when pressed.
3. Form the mixture into small balls, about the size of a walnut.
4. Preheat the air fryer to 200°C (390°F). Lightly spray the air fryer basket with olive oil.
5. Place the falafel balls in the basket, making sure they don't touch. Spray the falafel lightly with olive oil.
6. Cook for 10-15 minutes, shaking the basket halfway through, until the falafel are golden brown and crispy.
7. Serve hot with tahini sauce, hummus, or wrapped in pita bread with veggies.

Ingredients:
1. 1 can (15 oz) chickpeas, drained and rinsed
2. 1 small onion, chopped
3. 2 cloves garlic, minced
4. 1/4 cup fresh parsley, chopped
5. 2 tablespoons fresh cilantro, chopped (optional)
6. 1 teaspoon ground cumin
7. 1 teaspoon ground coriander
8. 1/2 teaspoon salt
9. 1/4 teaspoon black pepper
10. 1/4 teaspoon cayenne pepper (optional for heat)
11. 2 tablespoons all-purpose flour or chickpea flour
12. 1 teaspoon baking powder
13. Olive oil spray

*Calories: 200-250   Fat: 4-6g   Carbohydrates: 35-40g  Protein: 9-11g.   Fiber: 8-10g*

# Quick & Easy

## Bruschetta Chicken

*Prep: 10 min.     Cooking: 12-15 min.     Serves: 4*

*Instructions:*

1. Season the chicken breasts with salt and pepper. Drizzle with olive oil.
2. Preheat the air fryer to 180°C (350°F).
3. Place the chicken in the air fryer basket and cook for 10-12 minutes, flipping halfway through, until the chicken is cooked through and reaches an internal temperature of 74°C (165°F).
4. While the chicken is cooking, mix the diced tomatoes, chopped basil, minced garlic, and balsamic vinegar in a bowl to create the bruschetta topping.
5. Once the chicken is cooked, top each breast with the tomato mixture, and sprinkle with mozzarella cheese if using.
6. Return the chicken to the air fryer and cook for an additional 2-3 minutes, or until the cheese is melted and bubbly.
7. Serve the bruschetta chicken warm, garnished with extra basil if desired.

*Ingredients:*

1. 4 boneless, skinless chicken breasts
2. Salt and pepper to taste
3. 1 tablespoon olive oil
4. 2 medium tomatoes, diced
5. 1/4 cup fresh basil leaves, chopped
6. 2 cloves garlic, minced
7. 1 tablespoon balsamic vinegar
8. 1/4 cup shredded mozzarella cheese (optional)

*Calories: 220-270   Fat: 2-10g   Carbohydrates: 4-6g   Protein: 35-40g.   Fiber: 1-2g*

## Salmon with Lemon and Dill

*Prep: 5min.     Cooking: 10-12min.     Serves: 4*

*Instructions:*

1. Season the salmon fillets with salt and pepper. Drizzle with olive oil, lemon juice, and sprinkle with lemon zest and chopped dill.
2. Let the salmon marinate for a few minutes while you preheat the air fryer to 200°C (390°F).
3. Place lemon slices in the air fryer basket to create a bed for the salmon.
4. Lay the salmon fillets on top of the lemon slices, skin-side down.
5. Cook for 10-12 minutes, or until the salmon is cooked through and flakes easily with a fork.
6. Serve the salmon garnished with additional fresh dill and lemon wedges on the side.

*Ingredients:*

1. 4 salmon fillets (about 6 ounces each)
2. 2 lemons (1 zested and juiced, 1 sliced)
3. 2 tablespoons fresh dill, chopped, plus more for garnish
4. 2 tablespoons olive oil
5. Salt and pepper to taste

*Calories: 250-300   Fat: 15-20g   Carbohydrates: 2-3g   Protein: 23-28g.   Fiber: 0-1g*

# Quick & Easy

## Zucchini Fritters

*Prep: 15min.    Cooking: 10-15min.    Serves: 4*

*Instructions:*

1. In a large bowl, combine the grated zucchini, crumbled feta, chopped dill, flour, and egg. Season with salt and pepper, and mix well to form a batter.
2. Preheat the air fryer to 190°C (375°F) and lightly spray the basket with olive oil.
3. Form the zucchini mixture into small patties and place them in the air fryer basket, making sure they don't touch.
4. Cook for 10-15 minutes, flipping halfway through, until the fritters are golden brown and crispy.
5. While the fritters are cooking, prepare the tzatziki sauce by mixing the Greek yogurt, grated cucumber, minced garlic, olive oil, and dill in a bowl. Season with salt and lemon juice to taste.
6. Serve the zucchini fritters hot with the tzatziki sauce on the side.

*Ingredients:*
1. 2 medium zucchinis, grated and excess moisture squeezed out
2. 1/2 cup feta cheese, crumbled
3. 2 tablespoons fresh dill, chopped
4. 1/4 cup all-purpose flour
5. 1 egg
6. Salt and pepper to taste
7. Olive oil spray

*For the Tzatziki Sauce:*
8. 1 cup Greek yogurt
9. 1 small cucumber, grated and excess moisture squeezed out
10. 2 cloves garlic, minced
11. 1 tablespoon olive oil
12. 1 tablespoon fresh dill, chopped
13. Salt and lemon juice to taste

*Calories: 150-200   Fat: 8-10g   Carbohydrates: 10-15g   Protein: 8-10g.   Fiber: 1-2g*

## Caprese Salad Skewers

*Prep: 10 min       Cooking: No cooking required.    Serves: 4-6*

*Instructions:*

1. Skewer a cherry tomato, a basil leaf, and a mozzarella ball onto small cocktail sticks or skewers, repeating until all ingredients are used.
2. Arrange the skewers on a serving platter.
3. Drizzle with balsamic reduction, and season with salt and pepper. Optionally, you can drizzle a little olive oil over the skewers.
4. Serve immediately, offering the fresh and vibrant flavors of a Caprese salad in a fun, bite-sized form.

*Ingredients:*
1. Cherry tomatoes
2. Fresh mozzarella balls (bocconcini)
3. Fresh basil leaves
4. Balsamic reduction (or balsamic vinegar glaze)
5. Salt and pepper to taste
6. Olive oil (optional)

*Calories: Approximately 100-150.  Fat: 8-10g   Carbohydrates: 3-5g   Protein: 6-8g.   Fiber: 1g*

# Quick & Easy

## Stuffed Peppers

*Prep: 15min.      Cooking: 15-20 min.      Serves: 4*

*Instructions:*

1. In a bowl, mix the cooked rice, diced tomatoes, chopped olives, crumbled feta (if using), onion, garlic, olive oil, oregano, salt, and pepper to make the stuffing.
2. Stuff the mixture evenly into the hollowed-out bell peppers.
3. Preheat the air fryer to 180°C (350°F).
4. Place the stuffed peppers upright in the air fryer basket. If they wobble, you can trim the bottoms slightly to make them stand.
5. Cook for 15-20 minutes, or until the peppers are tender and the filling is heated through.
6. Serve the stuffed peppers hot, garnished with fresh herbs or a drizzle of olive oil if desired.

| Ingredients: |
| --- |
| 1. 4 bell peppers, tops cut off and seeds removed |
| 2. 1 cup cooked rice |
| 3. 1/2 cup diced tomatoes |
| 4. 1/2 cup chopped olives (green or black) |
| 5. 1/4 cup crumbled feta cheese (optional) |
| 6. 1 onion, finely chopped |
| 7. 2 cloves garlic, minced |
| 8. 2 tablespoons olive oil |
| 9. 1 teaspoon dried oregano |
| 10. Salt and pepper to taste |

*Calories: 220-250   Fat: 8-10g   Carbohydrates: 30-35g   Protein: 5-7g.   Fiber: 4-6g*

## Eggplant Parmesan Stacks

*Prep: 10min.      Cooking: 15-20 min.      Serves: 4*

*Instructions:*

1. Season the eggplant slices with salt and let them sit for a few minutes to draw out moisture, then pat dry.
2. Preheat the air fryer to 200°C (390°F) and lightly spray the basket with olive oil.
3. Place eggplant slices in the air fryer in a single layer and cook for 6-8 minutes, flipping halfway through, until they are tender and slightly golden.
4. Layer each eggplant slice with marinara sauce, mozzarella, and a sprinkle of Parmesan and oregano or Italian seasoning.

| Ingredients: |
| --- |
| 1. 1 large eggplant, sliced into 1/2 inch rounds |
| 2. Salt and pepper to taste |
| 3. 1 cup marinara sauce |
| 4. 1 cup shredded mozzarella cheese |
| 5. 1/4 cup grated Parmesan cheese |
| 6. 1 teaspoon dried oregano or Italian seasoning |
| 7. Olive oil spray |

5. Return the stacked eggplant slices to the air fryer and cook for another 5-7 minutes, or until the cheese is melted and bubbly.
6. Serve hot, garnished with fresh basil if desired.

*Calories: 200-250   Fat: 10-15g   Carbohydrates: 15-20g   Protein: 10-15g.   Fiber: 5-6g*

# Quick & Easy

## Shrimp and Asparagus

*Prep: 10min.     Cooking: 8-10min.     Serves: 4*

*Instructions:*

1. In a bowl, combine shrimp, asparagus, garlic, lemon zest, lemon juice, and olive oil. Season with salt, pepper, and red pepper flakes if using.
2. Toss everything together until well coated.
3. Preheat the air fryer to 200°C (390°F).
4. Place the shrimp and asparagus mixture in the air fryer basket in a single layer.
5. Cook for 8-10 minutes, shaking the basket halfway through, until the shrimp are pink and opaque and the asparagus is tender.
6. Serve immediately, garnished with additional lemon wedges or fresh herbs if desired.

*Ingredients:*

1. 1 lb (450 g) shrimp, peeled and deveined
2. 1 bunch of asparagus, trimmed and cut into pieces
3. 2 cloves garlic, minced
4. Zest and juice of 1 lemon
5. 2 tablespoons olive oil
6. Salt and pepper to taste
7. Optional: red pepper flakes for heat

*Calories: 200-250   Fat: 8-10g   Carbohydrates: 5-10g   Protein: 25-30g.   Fiber: 2-3g*

## Zucchini Fritters

*Prep: 15min.     Cooking: 10-15min.     Serves: 4*

*Instructions:*

7. In a large bowl, combine the grated zucchini, crumbled feta, chopped dill, flour, and egg. Season with salt and pepper, and mix well to form a batter.
8. Preheat the air fryer to 190°C (375°F) and lightly spray the basket with olive oil.
9. Form the zucchini mixture into small patties and place them in the air fryer basket, making sure they don't touch.
10. Cook for 10-15 minutes, flipping halfway through, until the fritters are golden brown and crispy.
11. While the fritters are cooking, prepare the tzatziki sauce by mixing the Greek yogurt, grated cucumber, minced garlic, olive oil, and dill in a bowl. Season with salt and lemon juice to taste.
12. Serve the zucchini fritters hot with the tzatziki sauce on the side.

*Ingredients:*

14. 2 medium zucchinis, grated and excess moisture squeezed out
15. 1/2 cup feta cheese, crumbled
16. 2 tablespoons fresh dill, chopped
17. 1/4 cup all-purpose flour
18. 1 egg
19. Salt and pepper to taste
20. Olive oil spray
21. For the Tzatziki Sauce:
22. 1 cup Greek yogurt
23. 1 small cucumber, grated and excess moisture squeezed out
24. 2 cloves garlic, minced
25. 1 tablespoon olive oil
26. 1 tablespoon fresh dill, chopped
27. Salt and lemon juice to taste

*Calories: 150-200   Fat: 8-10g   Carbohydrates: 10-15g   Protein: 8-10g.   Fiber: 1-2g*

# Quick & Easy

## Eggplant Parmesan Stacks

*Prep: 10min.     Cooking: 15-20 min.      Serves: 4*

*Instructions:*

7. Season the eggplant slices with salt and let them sit for a few minutes to draw out moisture, then pat dry.
8. Preheat the air fryer to 200°C (390°F) and lightly spray the basket with olive oil.
9. Place eggplant slices in the air fryer in a single layer and cook for 6-8 minutes, flipping halfway through, until they are tender and slightly golden.
10. Layer each eggplant slice with marinara sauce, mozzarella, and a sprinkle of Parmesan and oregano or Italian seasoning.
11. Return the stacked eggplant slices to the air fryer and cook for another 5-7 minutes, or until the cheese is melted and bubbly.
12. Serve hot, garnished with fresh basil if desired.

*Ingredients:*
8. 1 large eggplant, sliced into 1/2 inch rounds
9. Salt and pepper to taste
10. 1 cup marinara sauce
11. 1 cup shredded mozzarella cheese
12. 1/4 cup grated Parmesan cheese
13. 1 teaspoon dried oregano or Italian seasoning
14. Olive oil spray

*Calories: 150-200   Fat: 10-12g   Carbohydrates: 10-15g   Protein: 5-7g.   Fiber: 1-2g*

## Roast Potatoes

*Prep: 10min.     Cooking: 15-20min.     Serves: 4*

Instructions:
1. In a large bowl, toss the potatoes with olive oil, minced garlic, chopped rosemary, thyme, salt, and pepper until well coated.
2. Preheat the air fryer to 200°C (400°F).
3. Place the seasoned potatoes in the air fryer basket in a single layer.
4. Cook for 15-20 minutes, shaking the basket halfway through, until the potatoes are golden brown and crispy on the outside, and fork-tender on the inside.
5. Serve the potatoes hot, garnished with additional herbs if desired.

*Ingredients:*
8. 1 lb (450 g) baby potatoes, halved or quartered if large
9. 2 tablespoons olive oil
10. 2 cloves garlic, minced
11. 1 teaspoon fresh rosemary, chopped
12. 1 teaspoon fresh thyme, chopped
13. Salt and pepper to taste

*Calories: 200-250   Fat: 7-10g   Carbohydrates: 30-35g   Protein: 3-4g.   Fiber: 3-4g*

# Quick & Easy

## Chicken Shawarma

*Prep: 10min. (plus marinating time, ideally 30 minutes)     Cooking: 15-20 min.     Serves: 4*

*Instructions:*

1. In a bowl, mix the chicken with olive oil, Shawarma spices, and salt. Marinate for at least 30 minutes in the refrigerator.
2. Preheat the air fryer to 200°C (390°F).
3. Place the marinated chicken in the air fryer basket in a single layer.
4. Cook for 15-20 minutes, turning the pieces halfway through, until the chicken is golden brown and cooked through.
5. While the chicken is cooking, prepare the yogurt sauce by combining Greek yogurt, lemon juice, minced garlic, salt, pepper, and herbs in a bowl. Mix well.
6. Serve the Chicken Shawarma hot with the yogurt sauce on the side.

*Ingredients:*

1. 1 lb (450 g) chicken thighs, cut into strips
2. 2 tablespoons olive oil
3. 1 tablespoon Shawarma spice blend (combination of cumin, coriander, paprika, turmeric, garlic powder)
4. Salt to taste

*Ingredients for Yogurt Sauce:*

5. 1 cup Greek yogurt
6. 1 tablespoon lemon juice
7. 1 garlic clove, minced
8. Salt and pepper to taste
9. Fresh herbs (like parsley or mint), chopped

*Calories: 300-350   Fat: 15-20g   Carbohydrates: 5-10g   Protein: 35-40g.   Fiber: 1-2g*

## Spanakopita Bites

*Prep: 15min.     Cooking: 8-10min.     Serves: 4-6 (makes about 20 bites)*

*Instructions:*

1. Preheat the air fryer to 180°C (350°F).
2. In a bowl, mix the cooked spinach, crumbled feta, onions, minced garlic, olive oil, beaten egg, salt, pepper, and nutmeg until well combined.
3. Cut the phyllo dough into squares (around 4x4 inches).
4. Place a small spoonful of the spinach and feta mixture in the center of each phyllo square.
5. Brush the edges of the phyllo with olive oil, fold over the filling to form triangles or envelopes, and press the edges to seal.
6. Brush the outside of each spanakopita bite with olive oil.
7. Arrange the spanakopita bites in a single layer in the air fryer basket (cook in batches if necessary).
8. Cook for 8-10 minutes, or until golden brown and crispy.
9. Serve warm.

*Ingredients:*

1. 1 package phyllo dough, thawed
2. 2 cups spinach, cooked and squeezed dry
3. 1 cup feta cheese, crumbled
4. 1/4 cup onions, finely chopped
5. 1 garlic clove, minced
6. 2 tablespoons olive oil, plus extra for brushing
7. 1 egg, beaten
8. Salt and pepper to taste
9. Nutmeg (optional, a pinch for flavor)

*Calories: 150-200   Fat: 10-15g   Carbohydrates: 15-20g   Protein: 5-7g.   Fiber: 1-2g*

# Quick & Easy

## Lamb Kofta Kebabs

*Prep: 10min.    Cooking: 10-15 min.      Serves: 4*

*Instructions:*

1. In a large bowl, combine the ground lamb, grated onion, minced garlic, chopped parsley, cumin, coriander, cinnamon, paprika, salt, and pepper. Mix well.
2. Divide the mixture into equal portions and shape each into a long, thin kebab around skewers (if using wooden skewers, soak them in water for at least 30 minutes beforehand).
3. Preheat the air fryer to 200°C (390°F).
4. Place the kofta kebabs in the air fryer basket, ensuring they are not touching.
5. Cook for 10-15 minutes, turning halfway through, until the kebabs are well browned and cooked through.
6. Serve hot, garnished with fresh herbs or alongside a salad, yogurt sauce, or flatbread.

*Ingredients:*

1. 1 lb (450 g) ground lamb
2. 1 onion, finely grated
3. 2 cloves garlic, minced
4. 2 tablespoons fresh parsley, chopped
5. 1 teaspoon ground cumin
6. 1 teaspoon ground coriander
7. 1/2 teaspoon ground cinnamon
8. 1/2 teaspoon paprika
9. Salt and pepper to taste

*Calories: 300-350    Fat: 20-25g    Carbohydrates: 5-10g    Protein: 25-30g.    Fiber: 1g*

## Cauliflower Tabbouleh

*Prep: 10min.    Cooking: 10-15min.    Serves: 4-6*

*Instructions:*

1. Place cauliflower florets in a food processor and pulse until finely chopped and rice-like in texture.
2. Preheat the air fryer to 180°C (350°F).
3. Spread the chopped cauliflower in the air fryer basket and cook for 10-15 minutes, stirring halfway through, until slightly tender and golden. Let it cool.
4. In a large bowl, combine the cooled cauliflower, chopped parsley, mint, diced tomatoes, cucumber, lemon juice, olive oil, and minced garlic. Season with salt and pepper.
5. Toss everything together until well mixed and adjust seasoning to taste.
6. Chill in the refrigerator for at least 30 minutes before serving to allow the flavors to meld.

*Ingredients:*

1. 1 large head of cauliflower, cut into florets
2. 1 cup fresh parsley, finely chopped
3. 1/2 cup fresh mint, finely chopped
4. 2 tomatoes, diced
5. 1 cucumber, diced
6. 1/4 cup lemon juice
7. 1/4 cup olive oil
8. 2 cloves garlic, minced
9. Salt and pepper to taste

*Calories: 100-150    Fat: 7-10g    Carbohydrates: 10-15g    Protein: 2-4g.    Fiber: 3-5*

# Quick & Easy

## Mozzarella and Tomato Bites

*Prep: 10min.     Cooking: 5 min.  (just to warm through, if desired).     Serves: 4-6 (makes about 12-15 skewers)*

*Instructions:*

1. Skewer alternating cherry tomatoes, basil leaves (if using), and mini mozzarella balls onto small cocktail sticks or skewers.
2. If desired, lightly spray the skewers with olive oil and season with a pinch of salt and pepper.
3. Preheat the air fryer to 180°C (350°F).
4. Place the skewers in the air fryer basket. You can cook them briefly for about 2-5 minutes if you prefer the cheese to be slightly melted and the tomatoes warm, or serve them fresh as they are.
5. Drizzle the skewers with balsamic glaze before serving.

*Ingredients:*
1. Cherry tomatoes
2. Mini mozzarella cheese balls
3. Fresh basil leaves (optional)
4. Balsamic glaze
5. Salt and pepper to taste
6. Olive oil spray (if needed)

*Calories: 100-150   Fat: 7-9g   Carbohydrates: 3-5g   Protein: 6-8g.   Fiber: 1g*

## Pita Bread

*Prep: 15 min.  (plus 1 hour for dough to rise).     Cooking: 3-5 min.  per pita     Serves: 4-6*

*Instructions:*

1. In a mixing bowl, combine the flour, instant yeast, sugar, and salt.
2. Add the warm water and olive oil, and mix to form a soft, sticky dough.
3. Knead the dough on a floured surface for about 5 minutes until smooth.
4. Place the dough in a greased bowl, cover with a cloth, and let it rise in a warm place for about 1 hour, or until doubled in size.
5. After rising, punch down the dough and divide it into 4-6 equal pieces. Roll each piece into a ball, then flatten into discs about 1/4 inch thick.
6. Preheat the air fryer to 200°C (390°F).
7. Place one or two pieces of flattened dough in the air fryer basket (depending on size), and cook for 3-5 minutes, flipping halfway through, until puffed and lightly golden.
8. Repeat with the remaining dough.

*Ingredients:*
1. 2 cups all-purpose flour, plus extra for dusting
2. 1 teaspoon instant yeast
3. 1 teaspoon sugar
4. 1/2 teaspoon salt
5. 3/4 cup warm water
6. 1 tablespoon olive oil

*Calories: 180-220   Fat: 2-3g   Carbohydrates: 35-40g   Protein: 5-6g.   Fiber: 1-2g*

## Fish Fillets with Olives and Tomatoes

*Prep: 10min.     Cooking: 10-12min.     Serves: 4*

*Instructions:*

6. Season the fish fillets with salt, pepper, and oregano or Italian seasoning.
7. In a bowl, mix the cherry tomatoes, olives, minced garlic, and olive oil.
8. Preheat the air fryer to 200°C (390°F).
9. Place the fish fillets in the air fryer basket and top with the tomato and olive mixture.
10. Cook for 10-12 minutes, or until the fish is cooked through and flakes easily with a fork.
11. Serve the fish hot, garnished with lemon wedges.

*Ingredients:*
1. 4 fish fillets (such as cod, tilapia, or salmon)
2. 1 cup cherry tomatoes, halved
3. 1/2 cup olives, pitted and sliced
4. 2 tablespoons olive oil
5. 2 cloves garlic, minced
6. 1 teaspoon dried oregano or Italian seasoning
7. Salt and pepper to taste
8. Lemon wedges for serving

*Calories: 200-250   Fat: 10-12g   Carbohydrates: 5-7g   Protein: 25-30g.   Fiber: 1-2g*

## Garlic and Herb Roasted Chickpeas

*Prep: 5min.     Cooking: 10-15min.     Serves: 4*

*Instructions:*

1. In a bowl, toss the dried chickpeas with olive oil, garlic powder, dried herbs, salt, and pepper until evenly coated.
2. Preheat the air fryer to 200°C (390°F).
3. Spread the chickpeas in a single layer in the air fryer basket.
4. Cook for 15-20 minutes, shaking the basket every 5 minutes, until the chickpeas are golden brown and crispy.
5. Let them cool slightly before serving, as they will become crunchier as they cool.

*Calories: 150-200   Fat: 7-10g   Carbohydrates: 15-20g*
*Protein: 6-8g.   Fiber: 4-6g*

*Ingredients:*
1. 1 can (15 oz) chickpeas, drained, rinsed, and patted dry
2. 2 tablespoons olive oil
3. 1 teaspoon garlic powder
4. 1 teaspoon dried herbs (such as thyme, rosemary, or oregano)
5. Salt and pepper to taste

# Quick & Easy

## Vegetable and Feta Frittata

*Prep: 10min.      Cooking: 15-20min.      Serves: 4*

### Instructions:

1. In a bowl, whisk together the eggs, milk, salt, and pepper.
2. Stir in the crumbled feta cheese, chopped spinach, bell peppers, onions, tomatoes, and minced garlic.
3. Grease a round cake pan or an air fryer-safe dish with olive oil.
4. Pour the egg mixture into the prepared dish.
5. Preheat the air fryer to 180°C (350°F).
6. Place the dish in the air fryer basket and cook for 15-20 minutes, or until the frittata is set and lightly golden on top.
7. Check doneness by inserting a knife in the center; it should come out clean.
8. Serve warm, cut into wedges.

### Ingredients:
1. 6 eggs
2. 1/2 cup milk
3. 1/2 cup crumbled feta cheese
4. 1 cup chopped spinach
5. 1/2 cup diced bell peppers (various colors)
6. 1/4 cup diced onions
7. 1/4 cup chopped tomatoes
8. 1 garlic clove, minced
9. Salt and pepper to taste
10. 1 tablespoon olive oil

Calories: 250-300   Fat: 18-22g   Carbohydrates: 6-10g   Protein: 15-20g.   Fiber: 1-3g


## Herb Lemon Chicken Drumsticks

*Prep: 10 min. (plus marinating time, at least 30 min. or overnight)      Cooking: 20-25min.      Serves: 4*

### Instructions:

1. In a large bowl, whisk together lemon juice and zest, olive oil, minced garlic, chopped herbs, salt, and pepper to make the marinade.
2. Add the chicken drumsticks to the marinade, ensuring they are well coated. Cover and refrigerate for at least 30 minutes, or overnight for more flavor.
3. Preheat the air fryer to 200°C (390°F).
4. Place the marinated drumsticks in the air fryer basket, ensuring they are not overcrowded.
5. Cook for 20-25 minutes, turning the drumsticks halfway through, until they are golden brown and cooked through.
6. Serve hot, garnished with additional fresh herbs or lemon wedges if desired.

### Ingredients:
1. 8 chicken drumsticks
2. Juice and zest of 1 lemon
3. 1/4 cup olive oil
4. 2 cloves garlic, minced
5. 2 tablespoons fresh herbs (such as rosemary, thyme, and parsley), chopped
6. Salt and pepper to taste

Calories: 300-350   Fat: 15-20g   Carbohydrates: 1-3g   Protein: 35-40g.   Fiber: 0g

## Baked Feta with Tomatoes

*Prep: 5min.          Cooking: 15min.          Serves: 2-4*

*Instructions:*

8. Place the block of feta cheese in the center of a baking dish or foil tray that fits in your air fryer.
9. Surround the feta with cherry tomatoes. Drizzle olive oil over the cheese and tomatoes.
10. Sprinkle minced garlic, oregano or Italian seasoning, salt, and pepper evenly over the top.
11. Preheat the air fryer to 200°C (400°F).
12. Place the dish or tray in the air fryer basket and cook for about 15 minutes, or until the tomatoes are burst and the feta is soft and slightly golden.
13. Garnish with fresh basil before serving.

*Ingredients:*

1. 1 block of feta cheese (about 8 ounces)
2. 2 cups cherry tomatoes
3. 3 tablespoons olive oil
4. 2 garlic cloves, minced
5. 1 teaspoon dried oregano or Italian seasoning
6. Salt and pepper to taste
7. Fresh basil for garnish

*Calories: 250-300    Fat: 20-25g    Carbohydrates: 5-10g    Protein: 12-15g.    Fiber: 1-2g*

## Mediterranean Quinoa Patties

*Prep: 10 min          Cooking: 15min.          Serves: Makes about 8-10 patties*

*Instructions:*

1. In a large bowl, combine cooked quinoa, crumbled feta, chopped olives, sun-dried tomatoes, eggs, breadcrumbs or almond flour, and fresh herbs. Season with salt and pepper.
2. Mix well until the ingredients are evenly distributed and the mixture holds together when formed into patties.
3. Shape the mixture into small, round patties.
4. Preheat the air fryer to 190°C (375°F) and lightly spray the basket with olive oil.
5. Place the patties in the air fryer basket, making sure they don't touch each other.
6. Cook for 15 minutes, flipping halfway through, until the patties are golden brown and crispy on the outside.
7. Serve warm, possibly with a side of yogurt dip or tahini sauce.

*Ingredients:*

1. 2 cups cooked quinoa (cooled)
2. 1/2 cup feta cheese, crumbled
3. 1/4 cup olives, chopped
4. 1/4 cup sun-dried tomatoes, chopped
5. 2 eggs
6. 1/4 cup breadcrumbs or almond flour for binding
7. 1 tablespoon fresh herbs (such as parsley or basil), chopped
8. Salt and pepper to taste
9. Olive oil spray for cooking

*Calories: 100-150    Fat: 4-6g    Carbohydrates: 15-20g    Protein: 5-7g.    Fiber: 2-3g*

# Quick & Easy

## Green Beans with Almonds and Garlic

*Prep: 5min.        Cooking: 10-12min.        Serves: 4*

*Instructions:*
6. In a bowl, toss the green beans with olive oil, minced garlic, salt, and pepper.
7. Preheat the air fryer to 200°C (390°F).
8. Place the green beans in the air fryer basket in a single layer, and cook for about 8 minutes.
9. Add the sliced almonds to the basket with the green beans, tossing to combine.
10. Continue cooking for an additional 2-4 minutes, or until the green beans are tender and the almonds are lightly toasted.
11. Serve hot, with additional seasoning if desired.

*Ingredients:*
1. 1 lb (450 g) fresh green beans, trimmed
2. 1/4 cup sliced almonds
3. 2-3 garlic cloves, minced
4. 2 tablespoons olive oil
5. Salt and pepper to taste

*Calories: 100-150   Fat: 7-9g   Carbohydrates: 10-12g   Protein: 3-4g.   Fiber: 3-4g*

## Turkish Meatballs (Köfte)

*Prep: 15 min        Cooking: 10-15min.        Serves: 4*

*Instructions:*
1. In a bowl, combine the ground meat, grated onion, minced garlic, chopped parsley, cumin, paprika, salt, and pepper. Mix thoroughly.
2. Form the mixture into small, oval-shaped meatballs.
3. Preheat the air fryer to 200°C (390°F).
4. Place the meatballs in the air fryer basket, ensuring they are not touching.
5. Cook for 10-15 minutes, turning halfway through, until browned and cooked through.
6. For the sauce, combine Greek yogurt or tahini with lemon juice, minced garlic, and salt in a bowl, mixing well.
7. Serve the köfte hot with the yogurt or tahini sauce on the side.

*Ingredients:*
1. 1 lb (450 g) ground lamb or beef
2. 1 onion, finely grated
3. 2 cloves garlic, minced
4. 1/4 cup fresh parsley, chopped
5. 1 teaspoon ground cumin
6. 1 teaspoon paprika
7. Salt and pepper to taste

*For the Yogurt or Tahini Sauce:*
8. 1 cup Greek yogurt or tahini
9. 1 tablespoon lemon juice
10. 1 clove garlic, minced
11. Salt to taste

*Calories: 300-350   Fat: 20-25g   Carbohydrates: 5-10g  Protein: 25-30g.   Fiber: 0-1g*

## Artichokes with Lemon and Garlic

*Prep: 10min.      Cooking: 15-20min.      Serves: 2-4*

*Instructions:*

6. Prepare the artichokes by trimming the stems and cutting off the top 1/3 of each artichoke. Remove the tough outer leaves, and cut in half lengthwise. Scoop out the choke if necessary.
7. Rub the artichokes with lemon juice to prevent browning.
8. In a small bowl, mix the minced garlic, olive oil, salt, and pepper.
9. Brush the artichokes with the garlic and oil mixture, ensuring to get between the leaves.
10. Preheat the air fryer to 190°C (375°F).
11. Place the artichoke halves cut-side down in the air fryer basket, and scatter lemon slices around them.
12. Cook for 15-20 minutes, or until the artichokes are tender and the edges are slightly crispy.
13. Serve hot, with additional lemon wedges for squeezing.

*Ingredients:*
1. 2 large artichokes
2. 2 lemons (1 sliced, 1 juiced)
3. 4 cloves garlic, minced
4. 2 tablespoons olive oil
5. Salt and pepper to taste

*Calories: 150-200   Fat: 7-10g   Carbohydrates: 15-20g   Protein: 3-5g.   Fiber: 6-8g*

## Squid and Chorizo Tapas

*Prep: 10 min.      Cooking: 8-10min.      Serves: 2-4*

*Instructions:*

1. In a bowl, toss the squid rings and sliced chorizo with olive oil, smoked paprika, chili flakes (if using), minced garlic, salt, and pepper.
2. Preheat the air fryer to 200°C (390°F).
3. Spread the squid and chorizo mixture evenly in the air fryer basket.
4. Cook for 8-10 minutes, shaking the basket halfway through, until the squid is tender and the chorizo is slightly crisp.
5. Serve hot, garnished with chopped parsley.

*Ingredients:*
1. 1/2 lb (225 g) squid rings, cleaned
2. 1/2 lb (225 g) chorizo sausage, sliced
3. 1 tablespoon olive oil
4. 1 teaspoon smoked paprika
5. 1/2 teaspoon chili flakes (optional for extra heat)
6. 2 cloves garlic, minced
7. Salt and pepper to taste
8. Fresh parsley, chopped for garnish

*Calories: 250-300   Fat: 15-20g   Carbohydrates: 5-10g   Protein: 20-25g.   Fiber: 0-1g*

# Quick & Easy

## Prosciutto-Wrapped Asparagus

*Prep: 5min.      Cooking: 7-10min.      Serves: 4*

*Instructions:*

Ingredients:
1. 1 bunch of asparagus (about 16 spears), trimmed
2. 8 slices of prosciutto, halved lengthwise
3. Olive oil spray
4. Black pepper to taste

5. Wrap each asparagus spear with a strip of prosciutto, starting from the bottom to the top, leaving the tip exposed.
6. Lightly spray the wrapped asparagus with olive oil and season with black pepper.
7. Preheat the air fryer to 200°C (390°F).
8. Place the prosciutto-wrapped asparagus in the air fryer basket in a single layer, ensuring they are not overcrowded.
9. Cook for 7-10 minutes, or until the asparagus is tender and the prosciutto is crisp.
10. Serve immediately, perhaps with a drizzle of balsamic glaze or a squeeze of lemon for added flavor.

*Calories: 100-150   Fat: 6-8g   Carbohydrates: 3-5g   Protein: 10-12g.   Fiber: 1-2g*

## Greek Lemon and Herb Roasted Potatoes

*Prep: 10 min      Cooking: 15-20min.      Serves: 4*

*Instructions:*

Ingredients:
1. 1 lb (450 g) baby potatoes, halved or quartered
2. 2 tablespoons olive oil
3. Juice and zest of 1 lemon
4. 2 cloves garlic, minced
5. 1 teaspoon dried oregano
6. 1/2 teaspoon dried thyme
7. Salt and pepper to taste

1. In a large bowl, toss the potatoes with olive oil, lemon juice and zest, minced garlic, oregano, thyme, salt, and pepper until well coated.
2. Preheat the air fryer to 200°C (390°F).
3. Place the potatoes in the air fryer basket in a single layer.
4. Cook for 15-20 minutes, shaking the basket halfway through, until the potatoes are golden brown and tender.
5. Serve the potatoes hot, garnished with additional lemon zest or fresh herbs if desired.

*Calories: Approximately 200-250.  Fat: 7-10g   Carbohydrates: 30-35g   Protein: 4-5g.   Fiber: 4-5g*

# Lunch

Mediterranean Delights: Air Grill Lunch Creations

Indulge in the vibrant flavors and healthful ingredients of the Mediterranean with our enticing array of lunch recipes prepared on the air grill. From succulent meats to fresh vegetables, each dish captures the essence of this renowned culinary region, promising a tantalizing dining experience.

Start your Mediterranean feast with grilled vegetables bursting with flavor and nutrients. Imagine colorful bell peppers, zucchini, eggplant, and tomatoes, kissed by the flames of the air grill, imparting a delightful smokiness to every bite. Drizzled with a fragrant blend of olive oil, garlic, and herbs, these vegetables offer a tantalizing prelude to your main course.

For a heartier option, savor tender and juicy skewers of marinated meats, such as chicken, lamb, or beef, grilled to perfection. Infused with Mediterranean spices like oregano, thyme, and rosemary, each bite is a symphony of savory goodness. Paired with a refreshing tzatziki sauce or a tangy lemon-herb marinade, these grilled meats are sure to satisfy even the most discerning palate.

No Mediterranean-inspired lunch would be complete without the quintessential staple: fresh seafood. Delight in the delicate flavors of grilled fish, such as salmon, sea bass, or trout, expertly seasoned with lemon, garlic, and a sprinkle of sea salt. With its crispy exterior and moist, flaky flesh, each bite transports you to the sun-kissed shores of the Mediterranean coast.

Complement your meal with traditional Mediterranean sides, such as fluffy couscous, fragrant rice pilaf, or crispy Greek salad. Bursting with vibrant colors and bold flavors, these accompaniments add depth and variety to your culinary journey.

Finish your Mediterranean feast on a sweet note with a decadent dessert infused with Mediterranean flavors. Indulge in a slice of honey-drizzled baklava, or savor the creamy richness of Greek yogurt topped with fresh fruit and a sprinkle of nuts. Each bite is a celebration of the region's rich culinary heritage.

Whether you're hosting a leisurely lunch with friends or treating yourself to a solo dining experience, our Mediterranean-inspired recipes for the air grill are sure to elevate your mealtime to new heights. With their tantalizing flavors and healthful ingredients, these dishes offer a taste of the Mediterranean that's simply irresistible. Bon appétit!

## Lunch

# Lunch

## Greek Chicken Gyros

*Prep: 15min.      Cooking: 10-12min.      Serves: 4*

*Instructions:*

1. In a bowl, combine olive oil, minced garlic, oregano, paprika, lemon juice, salt, and pepper to create the marinade. Add the chicken strips and marinate for at least 30 minutes, preferably longer.
2. Preheat the air fryer to 200°C (390°F).
3. Place the marinated chicken strips in the air fryer basket and cook for 10-12 minutes, turning halfway through, until they are cooked through and golden.
4. While the chicken is cooking, prepare the tzatziki sauce by combining Greek yogurt, grated cucumber, minced garlic, olive oil, dill, lemon juice, and salt in a bowl. Mix well.
5. Warm the pita bread in the air fryer for about 1-2 minutes, if desired.
6. Assemble the gyros by placing chicken strips in the center of each pita, adding sliced tomatoes, onions, and lettuce, and topping with a generous dollop of tzatziki sauce.
7. Roll up the pita around the fillings and serve immediately.

*Ingredients:*
1. 1 lb (450 g) chicken breast, thinly sliced
2. 2 tablespoons olive oil
3. 2 garlic cloves, minced
4. 1 teaspoon dried oregano
5. 1/2 teaspoon paprika
6. Juice of 1 lemon
7. Salt and pepper to taste
8. Pita bread, for serving
9. Sliced tomatoes, onions, and lettuce for garnish

*For the Tzatziki Sauce:*
10. 1 cup Greek yogurt
11. 1/2 cucumber, grated and drained
12. 2 cloves garlic, minced
13. 1 tablespoon olive oil
14. 1 tablespoon fresh dill, chopped
15. Juice of 1/2 lemon
16. Salt to taste

*Calories: 400-500    Fat: 15-20g    Carbohydrates: 35-45g    Protein: 30-40g.    Fiber: 2-3g*

## Caprese Stuffed Avocados

*Prep: 10 min.      Cooking: 5-7min.      Serves: 4*

*Instructions:*

1. Scoop out a little avocado flesh to create space.
2. Mix chopped avocado with tomatoes, mozzarella, and basil.
3. Fill avocado halves with mixture.
4. Spray with olive oil, air fry at 180°C (350°F) for 5-7 minutes.
5. Drizzle with balsamic glaze before serving.

*Ingredients:*
1. 2 ripe avocados, halved and pitted
2. 1/2 cup cherry tomatoes, halved
3. 1/2 cup fresh mozzarella, diced
4. Fresh basil leaves
5. Balsamic glaze
6. Salt and pepper
7. Olive oil spray

*Calories: Approximately 250-300.  Fat: 20-25g. Carbohydrates: 12-15g   Protein: 7-10g.    Fiber: 6-7g*

# Lunch

## Falafel Wraps

*Prep: 20 min.      Cooking: 15min.      Serves: 4*

*Instructions:*

1. In a food processor, combine soaked chickpeas, onion, garlic, parsley, cumin, coriander, baking powder, salt, and pepper. Process until mixture is finely ground and holds together when pressed.
2. Form the mixture into small patties or balls.
3. Preheat the air fryer to 190°C (375°F) and lightly spray the basket with olive oil.
4. Place the falafel in the air fryer basket in a single layer, spray them lightly with olive oil, and cook for 15 minutes, flipping halfway through, until golden and crispy.
5. While the falafel cooks, prepare the tahini sauce by mixing tahini, lemon juice, minced garlic, salt, and water to achieve a drizzle-able consistency.
6. Warm the flatbread in the air fryer for 1-2 minutes if desired.
7. Assemble the wraps by placing lettuce, tomato, and cucumber slices on each flatbread, adding falafel, and drizzling with tahini sauce.
8. Roll up the flatbread around the fillings and serve.

Ingredients:
*For Falafel:*
1. 1 cup dried chickpeas, soaked overnight and drained
2. 1 small onion, chopped
3. 2 cloves garlic, minced
4. 1/4 cup fresh parsley, chopped
5. 1 teaspoon ground cumin
6. 1 teaspoon ground coriander
7. 1/2 teaspoon baking powder
8. Salt and pepper to taste
9. Olive oil spray

*For the Wraps:*
10. Flatbread or pita bread
11. Lettuce leaves
12. Tomato slices
13. Cucumber slices (optional)

*For the Tahini Sauce:*
14. 1/4 cup tahini
15. 2 tablespoons lemon juice
16. 1 clove garlic, minced
17. Water, as needed to thin
18. Salt to taste

*Calories: Approximately 400-450  Fat: 20-25g. Carbohydrates: 45-50g.  Protein: 13-15g. Fiber: 6-8g.*

## Mediterranean Shrimp Salad

*Prep: 10 min.      Cooking: 5-7min.      Serves: 4*

*Instructions:*

1. Preheat the air fryer to 200°C (390°F).
2. Toss shrimp with olive oil, salt, and pepper.
3. Air fry shrimp for 5-7 minutes until pink and cooked through.
4. In a large bowl, combine mixed greens, olives, and feta cheese.
5. Drizzle with olive oil and lemon juice, then toss to coat.
6. Top the salad with air-fried shrimp.
7. Serve immediately and enjoy!

Ingredients:
1. 1 lb shrimp, peeled and deveined
2. 4 cups mixed greens
3. 1/2 cup Kalamata olives, pitted
4. 1/2 cup crumbled feta cheese
5. Olive oil
6. Lemon juice
7. Salt and pepper

*Calories: Approximately 250-300.  Fat: 15-20g. Carbohydrates: 5-8g   Protein: 25-30g.    Fiber: 2-4g*

# Lunch

## Turkish Lamb Kofta

*Prep: 15 min.*        *Cooking: 10-12min.*     *Serves: Makes about 12 meatballs*

*Instructions:*

1. Preheat the air fryer to 180°C (360°F).
2. In a mixing bowl, combine ground lamb, chopped onion, minced garlic, chopped parsley, ground cumin, ground coriander, smoked paprika, salt, and pepper. Mix until well combined.
3. Shape the lamb mixture into small meatballs, about 1 inch in diameter.
4. Lightly brush or spray the meatballs with olive oil.
5. Place the meatballs in the air fryer basket in a single layer, making sure they are not touching.
6. Air fry the lamb kofta for 10-12 minutes, flipping halfway through, until golden brown and cooked through.
7. While the kofta is cooking, prepare the yogurt dip by mixing Greek yogurt with a pinch of salt.
8. Serve the air-fried lamb kofta hot with the yogurt dip on the side.

*Ingredients:*

1. 1 lb ground lamb
2. 1 small onion, finely chopped
3. 2 cloves garlic, minced
4. 2 tablespoons chopped fresh parsley
5. 1 teaspoon ground cumin
6. 1 teaspoon ground coriander
7. 1/2 teaspoon smoked paprika
8. Salt and pepper
9. Olive oil
10. Greek yogurt, for dipping

*Calories: Approximately 200-250  Fat: 15-20g. Carbohydrates: 1-2g.  Protein: 15-20g. Fiber: 0g.*

## Italian Eggplant Parmesan

*Prep: 15min.*        *Cooking: 10-12min.*     *Serves: 4*

*Instructions:*

1. Preheat the air fryer to 200°C (390°F).
2. In a shallow dish, mix breadcrumbs, grated Parmesan cheese, Italian seasoning, salt, and pepper.
3. Dip eggplant slices into beaten eggs, then coat them with the breadcrumb mixture, pressing gently to adhere.
4. Lightly spray or brush the coated eggplant slices with olive oil.
5. Arrange the coated eggplant slices in a single layer in the air fryer basket, ensuring they are not overlapping.
6. Air fry the eggplant slices for 10-12 minutes, flipping halfway through, until golden brown and crispy.
7. Serve the air-fried eggplant Parmesan slices hot with marinara sauce and garnish with fresh basil leaves.

Ingredients:

1. 1 large eggplant, sliced into rounds
2. 1 cup breadcrumbs
3. 1/2 cup grated Parmesan cheese
4. 2 eggs, beaten
5. 1 teaspoon Italian seasoning
6. Salt and pepper
7. Marinara sauce, for serving
8. Fresh basil leaves, for garnish

*Calories: Approximately 150-200  Fat: 5-8g. Carbohydrates: 20-25g   Protein: 6-8g.    Fiber: 5-7g*

# Lunch

## Moroccan Spiced Chicken

*Prep: 10 min.      Cooking: 20-30min.      Serves: 4*

*Instructions:*

1. Preheat the air fryer to 200°C (390°F).
2. In a small bowl, mix together olive oil, ground cumin, ground coriander, paprika, ground turmeric, ground cinnamon, ground ginger, salt, and pepper to form a spice paste.
3. Pat dry the chicken thighs with paper towels, then rub the spice paste all over the chicken, ensuring they are evenly coated.
4. Place the seasoned chicken thighs in the air fryer basket, skin side up, in a single layer, leaving space between each piece.
5. Air fry the chicken thighs for 25-30 minutes, or until the internal temperature reaches 75°C (165°F) and the skin is crispy and golden brown.
6. Remove the chicken thighs from the air fryer and let them rest for a few minutes before serving.
7. Serve the Moroccan Spiced Chicken hot with lemon wedges and garnish with fresh cilantro.

*Ingredients:*

1. 4 bone-in, skin-on chicken thighs
2. 2 tablespoons olive oil
3. 2 teaspoons ground cumin
4. 2 teaspoons ground coriander
5. 1 teaspoon paprika
6. 1 teaspoon ground turmeric
7. 1/2 teaspoon ground cinnamon
8. 1/2 teaspoon ground ginger
9. Salt and pepper
10. Lemon wedges, for serving
11. Fresh cilantro, for garnish

*Calories: Approximately 300-350  Fat: 20-25g. Carbohydrates: 2-3g.  Protein: 25-30g. Fiber: 1-2g.*

## Greek Lemon Potatoes

*Prep: 10min      Cooking: 25-30min.      Serves: 4*

*Instructions:*

1. Preheat the air fryer to 200°C (390°F).
2. In a large bowl, combine olive oil, minced garlic, lemon juice, dried oregano, dried thyme, salt, and pepper.
3. Add the potato wedges to the bowl and toss until evenly coated with the marinade.
4. Arrange the seasoned potato wedges in a single layer in the air fryer basket, ensuring they are not overcrowded.
5. Air fry the potato wedges for 25-30 minutes, shaking the basket halfway through, until they are golden brown and crispy on the outside and tender on the inside.
6. Remove the Greek Lemon Potatoes from the air fryer and transfer them to a serving dish.
7. Garnish with fresh parsley and serve hot as a delightful side dish to complement any meal.

*Ingredients:*

1. 4 medium potatoes, peeled and cut into wedges
2. 3 tablespoons olive oil
3. 2 cloves garlic, minced
4. 1 lemon, juiced
5. 1 teaspoon dried oregano
6. 1/2 teaspoon dried thyme
7. Salt and pepper
8. Fresh parsley, for garnish

*Calories: Approximately 150-200  Fat: 7-10g. Carbohydrates: 20-25g   Protein: 2-3g.   Fiber: 2-3g*

# Lunch

## Zucchini Fritters

*Prep: 15 min.        Cooking: 10-12min.        Serves: Makes about 8 fritters*

*Instructions:*

1. Preheat the air fryer to 200°C (390°F).
2. Place the grated zucchini in a clean kitchen towel and squeeze out excess moisture.
3. In a large bowl, combine the grated zucchini, crumbled feta cheese, chopped parsley, minced garlic, flour, beaten egg, salt, and pepper. Mix until well combined.
4. Form the zucchini mixture into small patties, about 2-3 inches in diameter.
5. Lightly spray the air fryer basket with olive oil spray. Arrange the zucchini fritters in a single layer in the basket, leaving some space between each fritter.

*Ingredients:*

1. 2 medium zucchinis, grated
2. 1/2 cup crumbled feta cheese
3. 1/4 cup chopped fresh parsley
4. 2 cloves garlic, minced
5. 1/4 cup all-purpose flour or almond flour
6. 1 egg, beaten
7. Salt and pepper
8. Olive oil spray

6. Air fry the fritters for 10-12 minutes, flipping halfway through, until they are golden brown and crispy on the outside.
7. Once cooked, remove the zucchini fritters from the air fryer and transfer them to a serving plate.
8. Serve the fritters hot as a delicious appetizer or side dish, optionally garnished with a dollop of Greek yogurt or tzatziki sauce.

*Calories: Approximately 100-120  Fat: 6-8g. Carbohydrates: 8-10g.  Protein: 4-5g. Fiber: 2-3g.*

## Spanish Chorizo and Potato Tapas

*Prep: 10min.        Cooking: 15-20min.        Serves: Makes 4 servings*

*Instructions:*

1. Preheat the air fryer to 200°C (390°F).
2. In a bowl, toss the halved baby potatoes with olive oil, salt, and pepper until evenly coated.
3. Arrange the seasoned potatoes and chorizo slices in a single layer in the air fryer basket.
4. Air fry for 15-20 minutes, shaking the basket halfway through, until the potatoes are tender and the chorizo is crispy.

*Ingredients:*

1. 10 baby potatoes, halved
2. 100g Spanish chorizo, sliced
3. 1 tablespoon olive oil
4. Salt and pepper, to taste
5. Wooden skewers, soaked in water for 30 minutes

5. While the potatoes and chorizo are air-frying, prepare the skewers by threading alternating pieces of potato and chorizo onto the soaked wooden skewers.
6. Once the potatoes and chorizo are cooked, remove them from the air fryer and let them cool slightly.
7. Skewer the air-fried potatoes and chorizo onto the prepared wooden skewers.
8. Serve the Spanish Chorizo and Potato Tapas warm as a delicious and flavorful appetizer or snack.

*Calories: Approximately 200-250  Fat: 10-15g. Carbohydrates: 15-20g   Protein: 8-10g.*

# Lunch

## Italian Prosciutto and Melon Recipe

*Prep: 10min.        Cooking: 5min.        Serves: 4*

Instructions:

1. Wrap the Melon: Wrap each piece of melon with a slice of prosciutto. The prosciutto should adhere to the melon's moisture.
2. Preheat the Air Fryer: Set the air fryer to 180°C (350°F).
3. Air-Fry the Melon: Place the wrapped melon pieces in the air fryer basket in a single layer. Air fry for 4-5 minutes, or until the prosciutto is slightly crisp.
4. Serve: Remove the prosciutto-wrapped melon from the air fryer and serve immediately while the prosciutto is crispy and the melon is warm.

Ingredients:
1. 1 cantaloupe or honeydew melon, cut into bite-sized pieces
2. 200g prosciutto slices

*Calories: Approximately 120   Protein: 7g.   Fat: 5g.   Carbohydrates: 15g. Fiber: 1g.*


## Veggie Pitas

*Prep: 15min.        Cooking: 12-15min.     Serves: Makes 2 servings*

Instructions:

1. Preheat the air fryer to 200°C (390°F).
2. In a large bowl, toss the sliced bell peppers, zucchini, and diced eggplant with olive oil, salt, and pepper until evenly coated.
3. Arrange the seasoned vegetables in a single layer in the air fryer basket.
4. Air fry the vegetables for 12-15 minutes, shaking the basket halfway through, until they are tender and lightly charred.
5. While the vegetables are air-frying, prepare the tahini sauce by whisking together tahini, lemon juice, minced garlic, and a splash of water until smooth. Adjust the consistency with more water if needed.
6. Warm the whole wheat pitas in the air fryer for 1-2 minutes until they are soft and pliable.

Ingredients:
6. 2 whole wheat pitas, halved
7. 1 red bell pepper, sliced
8. 1 yellow bell pepper, sliced
9. 1 small zucchini, sliced
10. 1 small eggplant, diced
11. 2 tablespoons olive oil
12. Salt and pepper
13. 2 tablespoons tahini
14. 1 tablespoon lemon juice
15. 2 cloves garlic, minced
16. Fresh parsley, for garnish

7. Once the vegetables are cooked, remove them from the air fryer and assemble the Mediterranean Veggie Pitas by stuffing each pita half with a generous portion of the air-fried vegetables.
8. Drizzle the tahini sauce over the stuffed pitas and garnish with fresh parsley.
9. Serve the Veggie Pitas warm as a delicious and nutritious lunch option.

*Calories: Approximately 300-350 Fat: 15-20g. Carbohydrates: 35-40g   Protein: 8-10g.    Fiber: 8-10g*

# Lunch

## Tuna Stuffed Bell Peppers

*Prep: 15min.          Cooking: 12-15min.*
*Serves: Makes 4 stuffed pepper halves*

Instructions:

1. Preheat the air fryer to 180°C (360°F).
2. In a mixing bowl, combine the drained tuna, diced cherry tomatoes, sliced black olives, finely chopped red onion, chopped parsley, lemon juice, olive oil, salt, and pepper. Mix well to combine.
3. Stuff each bell pepper half with the tuna salad mixture, pressing down gently to pack it in.
4. Place the stuffed bell pepper halves in the air fryer basket, arranging them in a single layer.
5. Air fry for 12-15 minutes, or until the bell peppers are tender and slightly charred on the edges.
6. Once cooked, remove the tuna stuffed bell peppers from the air fryer and let them cool slightly before serving.
7. Garnish with additional chopped parsley, if desired, and serve warm as a delicious and nutritious meal or appetizer.

*Ingredients:*
1. 2 bell peppers, halved and seeds removed
2. 1 can (5 oz) tuna, drained
3. 1/4 cup cherry tomatoes, diced
4. 2 tablespoons black olives, sliced
5. 2 tablespoons red onion, finely chopped
6. 1 tablespoon fresh parsley, chopped
7. 1 tablespoon lemon juice
8. 1 tablespoon olive oil
9. Salt and pepper, to taste

*Calories: Approximately 100-120 Fat: 5-7g. Carbohydrates: 5-7g  Protein: 10-12g.*

## Bruschetta

*Prep: 10min.          Cooking: 6-8min.      Serves: 4*

Instructions:

9. Preheat the air fryer to 180°C (350°F).
10. In a bowl, combine the diced tomatoes, minced garlic, chopped basil, and olive oil. Season with salt and pepper to taste, and toss until well combined.
11. Place the sliced bread in the air fryer basket in a single layer. You may need to do this in batches depending on the size of your air fryer.
12. Air fry the bread slices for 3-4 minutes, or until they are golden and crisp.
13. Once the bread is toasted, remove it from the air fryer and top each slice with the tomato mixture, dividing it evenly.
14. Return the topped bread slices to the air fryer basket and air fry for an additional 3-4 minutes, or until the tomatoes are slightly softened and warmed through.
15. Remove the bruschetta from the air fryer and transfer to a serving plate. Drizzle with extra olive oil and balsamic glaze, and sprinkle with grated Parmesan cheese if desired.
16. Serve immediately as a delicious appetizer or snack.

*Ingredients:*
1. 4 slices of crusty bread (baguette or Italian bread), sliced diagonally
2. 2 large tomatoes, diced
3. 2 cloves garlic, minced
4. 2 tablespoons chopped fresh basil
5. 1 tablespoon olive oil, plus extra for drizzling
6. Salt and pepper to taste
7. Balsamic glaze, for drizzling
8. Optional: grated Parmesan cheese for garnish

*Calories: Approximately 120-150 Fat: 4-6g. Carbohydrates: 15-20g  Protein: 3-5g.*

# Lunch

## Greek Meatball Pita Sandwiches

*Prep: 15min.        Cooking: 10-12min.        Serves: 4*

*Instructions:*

1. Mix ground meat, breadcrumbs, onion, garlic, oregano, mint, salt, and pepper.
2. Shape mixture into meatballs.
3. Air fry meatballs at 180°C for 10-12 mins, shaking halfway.
4. Mix yogurt, lemon juice, and dill.
5. Warm pita bread in air fryer.
6. Spread yogurt sauce inside each pita.
7. Fill with meatballs and cucumber slices.

*Calories: Approximately 400-450 Fat: 20-25g. Carbohydrates: 30-35g  Protein: 25-30g.*

*Ingredients:*
1. 1 lb ground lamb or beef
2. 1/2 cup breadcrumbs
3. 1/4 cup chopped onion
4. 2 cloves garlic, minced
5. 1 tsp dried oregano
6. 1 tsp dried mint
7. Salt and pepper
8. 4 pita bread rounds
9. 1 cucumber, sliced
10. 1/2 cup Greek yogurt
11. 1 tbsp lemon juice
12. 1 tbsp chopped fresh dill or mint

## Quinoa Bowls

*Prep: 10min.        Cooking: 15-20min.        Serves: Makes 4 servings*

*Instructions:*

1. In a medium saucepan, combine the rinsed quinoa and water or vegetable broth. Bring to a boil, then reduce heat to low, cover, and simmer for 15-20 minutes, or until the quinoa is cooked and the liquid is absorbed. Fluff with a fork and set aside.
2. While the quinoa is cooking, preheat the air fryer to 200°C (390°F).
3. In a mixing bowl, toss the sliced bell peppers, zucchini, red onion, and cherry tomatoes with olive oil until evenly coated. Season with salt and pepper to taste.
4. Place the seasoned vegetables in the air fryer basket in a single layer, ensuring they are not overcrowded. You may need to cook them in batches depending on the size of your air fryer.
5. Air fry the vegetables for 8-10 minutes, shaking the basket halfway through, until they are tender and lightly browned.
6. Divide the cooked quinoa among serving bowls. Top each bowl with a generous portion of the air-fried vegetables, Kalamata olives, and crumbled feta cheese.
7. Garnish with fresh parsley or basil, if desired, and serve immediately.

*Ingredients:*
1. 1 cup quinoa, rinsed
2. 2 cups water or vegetable broth
3. 1 tablespoon olive oil
4. 1 medium red bell pepper, sliced
5. 1 medium yellow bell pepper, sliced
6. 1 small zucchini, sliced
7. 1 small red onion, sliced
8. 1/2 cup cherry tomatoes, halved
9. 1/4 cup pitted Kalamata olives
10. 1/4 cup crumbled feta cheese
11. Salt and pepper to taste
12. Fresh parsley or basil, for garnish (optional)

*Calories: Approximately 300-350 Fat: 10-12g. Carbohydrates: 40-45g  Protein: 10-12g.*

# Lunch

## Fish Tacos Recipe

*Prep: 15min.       Cooking: 10min.       Serves: 4 (2 tacos each)*

Instructions:

1. Preheat the Air Fryer: Set the air fryer to 180°C (350°F).
2. Season the Fish: In a small bowl, mix olive oil, paprika, garlic powder, salt, and pepper. Brush the mixture over the fish fillets.
3. Cook the Fish: Place the fish in the air fryer basket. Cook for 10 minutes, or until the fish is cooked through and flaky.
4. Prepare the Slaw: While the fish is cooking, mix the shredded cabbage with Greek yogurt in a bowl. Season with salt and pepper to taste.
5. Assemble the Tacos: Warm the tortillas according to the package instructions. Place a portion of the fish on each tortilla, top with the Greek yogurt slaw, and add any optional garnishes.

*Ingredients:*

1. 4 white fish fillets (like cod or tilapia)
2. 1 cup Greek yogurt
3. 2 cups shredded cabbage (for slaw)
4. 1 tablespoon olive oil
5. 1 teaspoon paprika
6. 1 teaspoon garlic powder
7. Salt and pepper to taste
8. 8 small tortillas
9. Optional garnishes: chopped cilantro, lime wedges, sliced avocado

*Calories: Approximately 350 Fat: 15g. Carbohydrates: 35g  Protein: 25g.   Fiber: 5g.*


## Spiced Cauliflower Steaks Recipe

*Prep: 10min.       Cooking: 20min.       Serves: 4*

*Instructions:*

1. Prepare the Cauliflower: Remove the leaves and trim the stem of the cauliflower, keeping the core intact. Slice the cauliflower vertically into 1-inch thick steaks.
2. Season the Steaks: In a small bowl, mix olive oil, cumin, smoked paprika, garlic powder, salt, and pepper. Brush both sides of each cauliflower steak with the spice mixture.
3. Preheat the Air Fryer: Set the air fryer to 200°C (400°F).
4. Cook the Cauliflower: Place the seasoned cauliflower steaks in the air fryer basket in a single layer. Air fry for 10 minutes, flip, and continue cooking for another 10 minutes, or until the edges are crispy and the steaks are tender.
5. Serve: Garnish the cauliflower steaks with fresh herbs and serve hot.

*Ingredients:*

1. 1 large head of cauliflower
2. 2 tablespoons olive oil
3. 1 teaspoon cumin
4. 1 teaspoon smoked paprika
5. 1/2 teaspoon garlic powder
6. 1/2 teaspoon salt
7. 1/4 teaspoon black pepper
8. Fresh herbs (like parsley or cilantro) for garnish

*Calories: Approximately 120  Protein: 10-12g.  Fat: 10-12g. Carbohydrates: 12g. Fiber: 5g.*

# Lunch

## Israeli Sabich Sandwich Recipe

*Prep: 15min.        Cooking: 20min.        Serves: 4*

### Instructions:

1. Prepare the Eggplant: Brush the eggplant slices with olive oil and season with salt and pepper.
2. Cook the Eggplant: Preheat the air fryer to 200°C (400°F). Place the eggplant slices in the air fryer basket in a single layer. Cook for 10 minutes, flip, and continue cooking for another 10 minutes or until golden and tender.
3. Assemble the Sandwich: Slice open the pita breads but do not cut all the way through. Spread some tahini sauce inside each pita, then layer with the air-fried eggplant, boiled egg slices, tomato, cucumber, and onion.
4. Add Garnishes: Add parsley, pickles, and a drizzle of hot sauce if desired.
5. Serve: Enjoy the sabich sandwich immediately, with extra tahini sauce on the side if preferred.

> ### Ingredients:
> 1. 2 large eggplants, sliced
> 2. 4 eggs, boiled and sliced
> 3. 4 pita breads
> 4. 2 tomatoes, sliced
> 5. 1 cucumber, sliced
> 6. 1 small onion, sliced
> 7. 1 cup tahini sauce
> 8. Salt and pepper to taste
> 9. Olive oil for brushing
> 10. Optional: parsley, pickles, and hot sauce for garnish

*Calories: Approximately 450 Fat: 13g. Carbohydrates: 20g  Protein: 55g.   Fiber: 13g.*

## Lebanese Lentil Patties Recipe

*Prep: 15 min.  (plus time for cooking lentils if not pre-cooked)      Cooking: 20min.      Serves: 4*

### Instructions:

1. Prepare Lentil Mixture: In a large bowl, mash the cooked lentils. Add the onion, garlic, breadcrumbs, parsley, cumin, coriander, salt, and pepper. Mix well until the ingredients are combined and the mixture holds together.
2. Form the Patties: Divide the mixture into 8 equal portions. Shape each portion into a patty.
3. Preheat the Air Fryer: Set the air fryer to 190°C (375°F).
4. Cook the Patties: Brush both sides of each patty with olive oil. Place the patties in the air fryer basket in a single layer, ensuring they do not touch. Air fry for 10 minutes, flip, and continue cooking for another 10 minutes or until the patties are golden and crispy.
5. Serve: Serve the lentil patties hot, with a side of salad, yogurt sauce, or your favorite dipping sauce.

> ### Ingredients:
> 1. 2 cups cooked lentils (brown or green)
> 2. 1 small onion, finely chopped
> 3. 2 cloves garlic, minced
> 4. 1/2 cup breadcrumbs
> 5. 1/4 cup fresh parsley, chopped
> 6. 1 teaspoon ground cumin
> 7. 1 teaspoon ground coriander
> 8. Salt and pepper to taste
> 9. Olive oil for brushing

*Calories: Approximately 250  Protein: 14g.   Fat: 4g. Carbohydrates: 40g. Fiber: 16g.*

# Lunch

## Cypriot Halloumi and Vegetable Skewers Recipe

*Prep: 10min.      Cooking: 15min.      Serves: 4 skewers*

*Instructions:*

1. Prep the Ingredients: Thread the halloumi, bell pepper, zucchini, red onion, and cherry tomatoes onto skewers.
2. Season: Drizzle the skewers with olive oil and sprinkle with oregano, salt, and pepper.
3. Preheat the Air Fryer: Set the air fryer to 200°C (390°F).
4. Cook the Skewers: Place the skewers in the air fryer basket. Cook for 15 minutes, turning halfway through, or until the vegetables are tender and the halloumi is golden brown.
5. Serve: Remove the skewers from the air fryer and serve hot, with a side of fresh lemon wedges or dipping sauce if desired.

*Ingredients:*

1. 200g halloumi cheese, cut into cubes
2. 1 bell pepper, cut into chunks
3. 1 zucchini, cut into slices
4. 1 red onion, cut into chunks
5. 10 cherry tomatoes
6. 2 tablespoons olive oil
7. 1 teaspoon dried oregano
8. Salt and pepper to taste

*Calories: Approximately 250  Protein: 12g.  Fat: 18g.  Carbohydrates: 8g. Fiber: 2g.*

## Air-Fried Feta and Spinach Rolls Recipe

*Prep: 20min.      Cooking: 15min.      Serves: 4 (makes 8 rolls)*

*Instructions:*

1. Prepare the Filling: In a large bowl, mix the crumbled feta, chopped spinach, onion, garlic, salt, pepper, and nutmeg (if using) until well combined.
2. Assemble the Rolls: Lay a sheet of phyllo pastry flat on a clean surface. Brush lightly with olive oil. Place a portion of the feta and spinach mixture on one end of the sheet, then roll tightly to form a log. Repeat with the remaining phyllo sheets and filling.
3. Preheat the Air Fryer: Set the air fryer to 180°C (350°F).
4. Cook the Rolls: Brush the rolls with a little olive oil and place them in the air fryer basket, making sure they don't touch. Air fry for 15 minutes, turning halfway through, or until golden brown and crispy.
5. Serve: Let the rolls cool slightly before serving. They can be enjoyed hot or at room temperature.

*Ingredients:*

1. 200g feta cheese, crumbled
2. 2 cups fresh spinach, chopped
3. 1 small onion, finely chopped
4. 2 cloves garlic, minced
5. 4 sheets of phyllo pastry
6. 2 tablespoons olive oil
7. Salt and pepper to taste
8. 1 teaspoon nutmeg (optional)

*Calories: Approximately 300  Protein: 12g.  Fat: 18g.  Carbohydrates: 24g. Fiber: 2g.*

# Lunch

## Sicilian Caponata Recipe

*Prep: 15min.        Cooking: 20min.        Serves: 4*

*Instructions:*

1. Prepare the Vegetables: Toss the eggplant cubes with olive oil, salt, and pepper.
2. Cook the Eggplant: Preheat the air fryer to 200°C (390°F). Place the eggplant in the air fryer basket and cook for 10 minutes, shaking the basket halfway through.
3. Add Other Ingredients: In a bowl, mix the roasted eggplant with tomatoes, onion, garlic, capers, and olives.
4. Make the Sauce: In a small bowl, combine red wine vinegar, sugar, and dried basil. Pour this over the vegetable mixture and mix well.
5. Chill: Let the caponata sit for a few hours in the fridge to allow the flavors to meld.
6. Serve: Garnish with fresh basil or parsley before serving cold.

*Calories: Approximately 150   Protein: 2g.   Fat: 9g.*
*Carbohydrates: 18g. Fiber: 6g.*

*Ingredients:*

1. 1 large eggplant, cut into cubes
2. 2 tomatoes, chopped
3. 1 onion, chopped
4. 2 cloves of garlic, minced
5. 1/4 cup capers, rinsed
6. 1/4 cup green olives, sliced
7. 2 tablespoons olive oil
8. 2 tablespoons red wine vinegar
9. 1 tablespoon sugar
10. 1 teaspoon dried basil
11. Salt and pepper to taste
12. Fresh basil or parsley for garnish

## Stuffed Grape Leaves (Dolmas) Recipe

*Prep: 30min.        Cooking: 15min.        Serves: 5 (6 dolmas each)*

*Instructions:*

1. Prepare the Filling: In a bowl, mix the cooked rice, dill, parsley, onion, half of the olive oil, lemon juice, salt, and pepper.
2. Stuff the Leaves: Lay a grape leaf flat on a work surface, shiny side down. Place a spoonful of the rice mixture near the stem end. Fold in the sides and roll the leaf tightly around the filling. Repeat with the remaining leaves and filling.
3. Preheat the Air Fryer: Set the air fryer to 180°C (350°F).
4. Cook the Dolmas: Brush the dolmas with the remaining olive oil and place them in the air fryer basket in a single layer. Cook for 15 minutes, turning halfway through, until slightly crispy on the outside.
5. Serve: Let the dolmas cool slightly before serving. They can be enjoyed warm or at room temperature.

*Ingredients:*

1. 30 grape leaves, rinsed and drained
2. 1 cup cooked rice
3. 1/4 cup fresh dill, chopped
4. 1/4 cup fresh parsley, chopped
5. 1 onion, finely chopped
6. 2 tablespoons olive oil
7. 1 lemon, juiced
8. Salt and pepper to taste

*Calories: Approximately 150   Protein: 3g.   Fat: 5g.  Carbohydrates: 23g. Fiber: 3g.*

# Lunch

## Chicken Souvlaki Skewers

*Prep: 10min.        Cooking: 10-12min.        Serves: Makes 4 skewers*

*Instructions:*

11. In a bowl, combine the olive oil, minced garlic, dried oregano, dried thyme, paprika, salt, pepper, and lemon juice. Mix well to create the marinade.
12. Add the cubed chicken breast to the marinade and    toss until evenly coated. Cover the bowl and let the chicken marinate in the refrigerator for at least 30 minutes, or up to overnight.
13. Preheat the air fryer to 200°C (390°F).
14. Thread the marinated chicken cubes onto the soaked wooden skewers, distributing them evenly.
15. Place the chicken skewers in the air fryer basket, ensuring they are not touching each other.
16. Air fry for 10-12 minutes, flipping halfway through, until the chicken is cooked through and golden brown on the outside.
17. Once cooked, remove the chicken souvlaki skewers from the air fryer and let them rest for a few minutes before serving.
18. Serve the chicken souvlaki skewers with tzatziki sauce, pita bread, and your favorite Mediterranean sides.

*Ingredients:*

1. 2 boneless, skinless chicken breasts, cut into cubes
2. 2 tablespoons olive oil
3. 2 cloves garlic, minced
4. 1 teaspoon dried oregano
5. 1/2 teaspoon dried thyme
6. 1/2 teaspoon paprika
7. 1/2 teaspoon salt
8. 1/4 teaspoon black pepper
9. Juice of 1 lemon
10. Wooden skewers, soaked in water for 30 minutes

*Calories: Approximately 150-180  Fat: 7-9g. Carbohydrates: 1-2g  Protein: 20-25g.*

## Chicken and Orzo Salad Recipe

*Prep: 15min.      Cooking: 20min.      Serves: 4*

*Instructions:*

1. Cook the Chicken: Season the chicken breasts with salt, pepper, and a drizzle of olive oil. Preheat the air fryer to 180°C (350°F). Cook the chicken in the air fryer for 20 minutes, flipping halfway through, or until fully cooked and golden brown. Let it cool, then dice or shred it.
2. Prepare the Salad: In a large bowl, combine the cooked orzo, cherry tomatoes, cucumber, red onion, olives, and feta cheese.
3. Make the Dressing: In a small bowl, whisk together the lemon juice, olive oil, oregano, salt, and pepper.
4. Combine: Add the diced chicken to the salad bowl, pour over the dressing, and toss to combine everything well.
5. Serve: Enjoy the salad immediately, or chill it in the refrigerator for an hour before serving to enhance the flavors.

*Ingredients:*

1. 2 chicken breasts
2. 1 cup orzo pasta, cooked
3. 1 cup cherry tomatoes, halved
4. 1 cucumber, diced
5. 1/4 cup red onion, finely chopped
6. 1/4 cup kalamata olives, sliced
7. 1/4 cup feta cheese, crumbled
8. 2 tablespoons olive oil
9. 1 lemon, juiced
10. 1 teaspoon dried oregano
11. Salt and pepper to taste

*Calories: Approximately 400  Protein: 28g.  Fat: 15g. Carbohydrates: 40g. Fiber: 3g.*

# Lunch

## Greek Zucchini Balls Recipe

*Prep: 20 min. (including time to drain zucchini)*      *Cooking: 15min.*    *Serves: 4 (makes around 16 balls)*

*Instructions:*

10. Drain the Zucchini: Place the grated zucchini in a colander, sprinkle with salt, and let it sit for 10-15 minutes to draw out the moisture. Squeeze out the excess water.
11. Prepare the Mixture: In a bowl, combine the drained zucchini, feta cheese, breadcrumbs, egg, dill, mint, garlic, salt, and pepper. Mix well to form a cohesive mixture.
12. Form the Balls: Shape the mixture into small balls, about the size of a walnut.
13. Preheat the Air Fryer: Set the air fryer to 190°C (375°F).
14. Cook the Zucchini Balls: Brush the air fryer basket with olive oil and place the balls in the basket, making sure they are not touching. Brush the balls with a bit more olive oil. Air fry for 15 minutes, turning halfway through, until golden brown and crispy.
15. Serve: Serve the zucchini balls hot, with a side of tzatziki or Greek yogurt for dipping.

*Ingredients:*

1. 3 medium zucchinis, grated
2. 1 cup feta cheese, crumbled
3. 1/2 cup breadcrumbs
4. 1 egg
5. 2 tablespoons fresh dill, chopped
6. 2 tablespoons fresh mint, chopped
7. 1 clove garlic, minced
8. Salt and pepper to taste
9. Olive oil for brushing

*Calories: Approximately 200  Protein: 10g.   Fat: 10g.  Carbohydrates: 18g. Fiber: 3g.*

## Bean Salad Recipe

*Prep: 15min.*      *Cooking: 0 min.*      *Serves: 6*

*Instructions:*

1. Prepare the Salad: In a large bowl, combine the chickpeas, black beans, kidney beans, red bell pepper, cucumber, red onion, and parsley.
2. Make the Dressing: In a small bowl, whisk together the olive oil, lemon juice, minced garlic, salt, pepper, and oregano.
3. Combine: Pour the dressing over the salad and toss to coat all the ingredients evenly.
4. Chill and Serve: For the best flavor, let the salad chill in the refrigerator for at least 30 minutes before serving. This allows the flavors to meld together.

*Ingredients:*

1. 1 can (15 oz) chickpeas, drained and rinsed
2. 1 can (15 oz) black beans, drained and rinsed
3. 1 can (15 oz) kidney beans, drained and rinsed
4. 1 red bell pepper, diced
5. 1 cucumber, diced
6. 1 red onion, diced
7. 1/4 cup fresh parsley, chopped
8. 1/4 cup olive oil
9. 2 lemons, juiced
10. 1 garlic clove, minced
11. Salt and pepper to taste
12. 1 teaspoon dried oregano

*Calories: Approximately 250  Protein: 10g.   Fat: 8g. Carbohydrates: 35g. Fiber: 10g.*

# Lunch

## Portuguese Piri Piri Chicken Recipe

*Prep: 20 min. (plus marinating time if possible)    Cooking: 25min.    Serves: 4*

*Instructions:*

11. Marinate the Chicken: Coat the chicken with Piri Piri sauce, olive oil, and salt. Let it marinate for at least minutes if time allows.
12. Preheat the Air Fryer: Set the air fryer to 190°C (375°F).
13. Cook the Chicken: Place the chicken in the air fryer basket. Cook for 25 minutes, or until the chicken is cooked through and has a crispy exterior, turning halfway through.
14. Prepare the Cucumber Salad: Combine the cucumber, red onion, white wine vinegar, olive oil, pepper, and fresh herbs in a bowl. Toss to combine chill until ready to serve.
15. Serve: Place the cooked Piri Piri chicken on a plate serve with the chilled cucumber salad on the side.

*Calories: Approximately 350  Protein: 25g.   Fat: 20g. Carbohydrates: 5g. Fiber: 1g.*

*Ingredients:*

1. 4 chicken thighs or breasts
2. 2 tablespoons Piri Piri sauce (or make a mix of chili, paprika, garlic, olive oil, and lemon juice)    30
3. 1 tablespoon olive oil
4. Salt to taste

*For the cucumber salad:*

5. 1 large cucumber, thinly sliced
6. 1/4 red onion, thinly sliced    salt,
7. 2 tablespoons white wine vinegar    and
8. 1 tablespoon olive oil    and
9. Salt and pepper to taste
10. Fresh dill or parsley, chopped (optional)

## Italian Sausage and Peppers Recipe

*Prep: 10min.    Cooking: 20min.    Serves: 4*

*Instructions:*

1. Prep the Ingredients: Toss the sliced bell peppers and onion with olive oil, salt, pepper, and oregano in a bowl.
2. Preheat the Air Fryer: Set the air fryer to 180°C (350°F).
3. Cook the Sausage and Vegetables: Place the sausages in the air fryer basket. Add the seasoned peppers and onions around the sausages. Cook for 20 minutes, turning the sausages and stirring the vegetables halfway through, until the sausages are cooked through and the vegetables are tender and slightly caramelized.
4. Serve: Slice the sausages if desired and serve hot with the cooked peppers and onions.

*Calories: Approximately 400  Protein: 20g.   Fat: 30g.  Carbohydrates: 10g. Fiber: 2g.*

*Ingredients:*

1. 4 Italian sausages (about 400g)
2. 2 bell peppers, sliced
3. 1 large onion, sliced
4. 2 tablespoons olive oil
5. Salt and pepper to taste
6. 1 teaspoon dried oregano or Italian seasoning

# Lunch

## Balsamic Glazed Brussels Sprouts Recipe

*Prep: 10 min.*        *Cooking: 20min.*        *Serves: 4*

*Instructions:*

6. Prep the Brussels Sprouts: Toss the Brussels sprouts with olive oil, salt, and pepper.
7. Preheat the Air Fryer: Set the air fryer to 200°C (390°F).
8. Cook the Brussels Sprouts: Place the Brussels sprouts in the air fryer basket. Air fry for about 15-20 minutes, shaking the basket halfway through, until they are crispy and golden brown.
9. Prepare the Balsamic Glaze: While the Brussels sprouts are cooking, simmer the balsamic vinegar and honey (or brown sugar) in a small saucepan over medium heat until it reduces to a thick glaze, about 5 minutes.
10. Serve: Drizzle the balsamic glaze over the cooked Brussels sprouts and toss to coat evenly. Serve warm.

*Ingredients:*

1. 500g Brussels sprouts, trimmed and halved
2. 2 tablespoons olive oil
3. Salt and pepper to taste
4. 1/4 cup balsamic vinegar
5. 2 tablespoons honey or brown sugar

*Calories: Approximately 150  Protein: 4g.   Fat: 7g.  Carbohydrates: 20g. Fiber: 4g.*

## Italian Sausage and Peppers Recipe

*Prep: 10min.*        *Cooking: 20min.*        *Serves: 4*

*Instructions:*

5. Prep the Ingredients: Toss the sliced bell peppers and onion with olive oil, salt, pepper, and oregano in a bowl.
6. Preheat the Air Fryer: Set the air fryer to 180°C (350°F).
7. Cook the Sausage and Vegetables: Place the sausages in the air fryer basket. Add the seasoned peppers and onions around the sausages. Cook for 20 minutes, turning the sausages and stirring the vegetables halfway through, until the sausages are cooked through and the vegetables are tender and slightly caramelized.
8. Serve: Slice the sausages if desired and serve hot with the cooked peppers and onions.

*Ingredients:*

7. 4 Italian sausages (about 400g)
8. 2 bell peppers, sliced
9. 1 large onion, sliced
10. 2 tablespoons olive oil
11. Salt and pepper to taste
12. 1 teaspoon dried oregano or Italian seasoning

*Calories: Approximately 400  Protein: 20g.   Fat: 30g.  Carbohydrates: 10g. Fiber: 2g.*

# Lunch

## Greek-Style Pork Chops Recipe

*Prep: 10 min. (plus marinating time)      Cooking: 15min.      Serves: 4*

Instructions:

7. Marinate the Pork Chops: In a bowl, whisk together olive oil, lemon juice, garlic, oregano, salt, and pepper. Place the pork chops in a large resealable or shallow dish and pour the marinade over them. Ensure all sides are coated. Marinate in the refrigerator for at least 1 hour, preferably longer for more flavor.
8. Preheat the Air Fryer: Set the air fryer to 200°C (390°F).
9. Cook the Pork Chops: Remove the pork chops from the marinade and place them in the air fryer basket. Air fry for 15 minutes, flipping halfway through, or until the internal temperature reaches 63°C (145°F) and they are nicely browned.
10. Rest and Serve: Let the pork chops rest for a few minutes after cooking to allow the juices to redistribute. Serve with additional lemon slices and a sprinkle of fresh oregano if desired.

*Ingredients:*
1. 4 pork chops, bone-in or boneless
2. 1/4 cup olive oil
3. 2 lemons, juiced
4. 2 cloves garlic, minced
5. 1 tablespoon dried oregano
6. Salt and pepper to taste

bag

*Calories: Approximately 300  Protein: 30g.   Fat: 18g.  Carbohydrates: 2g. Fiber: 0g.*

## Moroccan Carrot Salad Recipe

*Prep: 15min.      Cooking: 20min.      Serves: 4*

Instructions:

1. Season the Carrots: Toss the carrots with half of the olive oil, cumin, cinnamon, ginger, salt, and pepper.
2. Air Fry the Carrots: Preheat the air fryer to 200°C (390°F). Cook the seasoned carrots for 20 minutes, shaking the basket halfway through, until they are tender and slightly caramelized.
3. Prepare the Dressing: Whisk together the lemon juice, remaining olive oil, honey, and minced garlic to make the dressing.
4. Assemble the Salad: In a large bowl, combine the air-fried carrots with the raisins, almonds, and parsley. Drizzle with the dressing and toss to combine.
5. Serve: Enjoy the salad warm or at room temperature.

*Ingredients:*
1. 500g carrots, peeled and sliced
2. 1/4 cup olive oil, divided
3. 1 teaspoon ground cumin
4. 1 teaspoon ground cinnamon
5. 1/2 teaspoon ground ginger
6. Salt and pepper to taste
7. 1/4 cup raisins
8. 1/4 cup almonds, toasted and chopped
9. 2 tablespoons fresh parsley, chopped
10. For the dressing:
11. 2 tablespoons lemon juice
12. 1 tablespoon honey
13. 1 clove garlic, minced

*Calories: Approximately 250  Protein: 3g.   Fat: 15g. Carbohydrates: 30g. Fiber: 6g.*

# Lunch

## Stuffed Zucchini Recipe

*Prep: 15 min.      Cooking: 20min.      Serves: 4*

*Instructions:*

12. Prepare the Zucchini: Scoop out the center of each zucchini half to create a "boat," leaving a border around the edges.
13. Make the Filling: In a bowl, combine the cooked quinoa or rice, cherry tomatoes, feta cheese, olives, onion, garlic, 1 tablespoon of olive oil, oregano, salt, and pepper.
14. Stuff the Zucchini: Spoon the filling into the zucchini boats, pressing down slightly to pack the filling.
15. Preheat the Air Fryer: Set the air fryer to 180°C (350°F).
16. Cook the Zucchini: Brush the zucchini boats with the remaining olive oil and place them in the air fryer basket. Cook for 20 minutes, or until the zucchini is tender and the top is slightly golden.
17. Serve: Garnish with fresh parsley before serving.

*Calories: Approximately 200  Protein: 6g.   Fat: 10g. Carbohydrates: 24g. Fiber: 5g.*

*Ingredients:*

1. 4 medium zucchinis, halved lengthwise
2. 1 cup cooked quinoa or rice
3. 1/2 cup cherry tomatoes, chopped
4. 1/4 cup feta cheese, crumbled
5. 1/4 cup black olives, chopped
6. 1 small onion, finely chopped
7. 2 cloves garlic, minced
8. 2 tablespoons olive oil
9. 1 teaspoon dried oregano
10. Salt and pepper to taste
11. Fresh parsley, for garnish

## Shakshuka-Style Eggs Recipe

*Prep: 10min.      Cooking: 20min.      Serves: 2*

*Instructions:*

1. Prep the Vegetables: In a bowl, mix the bell pepper, tomatoes, onion, garlic, paprika, cumin, salt, pepper, and olive oil.
2. Cook the Vegetables: Preheat the air fryer to 200°C (390°F). Place the vegetable mixture in the air fryer basket and cook for 10 minutes, until the vegetables are tender and slightly charred.
3. Add the Eggs: Make small wells in the cooked vegetables and carefully crack an egg into each well.
4. Continue Cooking: Return the basket to the air fryer and cook for another 8-10 minutes, or until the eggs are cooked to your liking.
5. Serve: Garnish with fresh parsley or cilantro before serving.

*Calories: Approximately 300  Protein: 14g.   Fat: 22g.  Carbohydrates: 12g. Fiber: 3g.*

*Ingredients:*

1. 4 large eggs
2. 1 bell pepper, sliced
3. 2 tomatoes, chopped
4. 1 small onion, chopped
5. 2 cloves garlic, minced
6. 1 teaspoon paprika
7. 1 teaspoon cumin
8. Salt and pepper to taste
9. 2 tablespoons olive oil
10. Fresh parsley or cilantro for garnish

# Lunch

## Spanish Potato Omelette (Tortilla Española) Recipe

*Prep: 15 min.        Cooking: 25min.        Serves: 4*

*Instructions:*

6. Prep the Potatoes and Onions: Toss the sliced potatoes and onions with half of the olive oil, salt, pepper.
7. Cook in the Air Fryer: Preheat the air fryer to 180°C (350°F). Place the potato and onion mixture in the air fryer basket and cook for 15-20 minutes, or until the potatoes are tender and lightly browned, stirring halfway through.
8. Prepare the Eggs: While the potatoes and onions are cooking, beat the eggs in a large bowl and season with salt and pepper.
9. Combine and Cook: Once the potatoes and onions are cooked, gently fold them into the beaten eggs. Heat the remaining olive oil in a large non-stick skillet over medium heat. Pour in the egg mixture, spreading the potatoes and onions evenly. Cook for a few minutes until the edges start to set, then reduce the heat to low and cook until the bottom is golden and the top is set.
10. Flip and Finish Cooking: Carefully flip the omelette using a large plate or lid and cook the other side until golden brown and fully set.
11. Serve: Slice the tortilla into wedges and serve warm or at room temperature.

*Ingredients:*
1. 3 large potatoes, thinly sliced
2. 1 large onion, thinly sliced
3. 6 large eggs
4. 1/4 cup olive oil
5. Salt and pepper to taste

and

*Calories: Approximately 300  Protein: 12g.   Fat: 18g.  Carbohydrates: 20g. Fiber: 3g.*

## Italian Antipasto Platter Recipe

*Prep: 20min.        Cooking: 15min.        Serves: 4-6*

*Instructions:*

1. Prepare the Vegetables: Toss the vegetables with olive oil, salt, pepper, and Italian seasoning.
2. Air Fry the Vegetables: Preheat the air fryer to 200°C (390°F). Cook the seasoned vegetables in batches for 10-15 minutes or until tender and slightly charred, stirring halfway through.
3. Assemble the Platter: Arrange the air-fried vegetables, meats, cheeses, olives, and pickled vegetables on a large serving platter.
4. Serve: Offer with slices of crusty bread, olive oil for dipping, and balsamic vinegar if desired.

*Ingredients:*
1. Assorted vegetables (like zucchini, bell peppers, cherry tomatoes, and mushrooms), cut into bite-sized pieces
2. Italian meats (such as salami, prosciutto, and capicola)
3. Assorted cheeses (like mozzarella, provolone, and parmesan)
4. Olives and pickled vegetables
5. Olive oil
6. Salt, pepper, and Italian seasoning for the vegetables

*Calories: Varies   Protein: Varies.   Fat: Varies.      Carbohydrates: Varies.    Fiber: Varies.*

# Lunch

## Roasted Chickpeas Recipe

*Prep: 5 min.        Cooking: 15min.        Serves: 4*

*Instructions:*

8. Prepare the Chickpeas: Ensure the chickpeas are dry by patting them with a paper towel. This helps to achieve a crispy texture when air-fried.
9. Season the Chickpeas: In a bowl, toss the chickpeas with olive oil, paprika, cumin, garlic powder, onion powder, salt, and pepper until evenly coated.
10. Preheat the Air Fryer: Set the air fryer to 200°C (390°F).
11. Cook the Chickpeas: Spread the chickpeas in a single layer in the air fryer basket. Air fry for 15 minutes, shaking the basket halfway through the cooking time, until they are golden brown and crispy.
12. Serve: Enjoy the chickpeas warm as a snack, or use them as a topping for salads or soups.

*Ingredients:*

1. 2 cups cooked chickpeas (or 1 can, drained and rinsed)
2. 2 tablespoons olive oil
3. 1 teaspoon paprika
4. 1 teaspoon ground cumin
5. 1/2 teaspoon garlic powder
6. 1/2 teaspoon onion powder
7. Salt and pepper to taste

*Calories: Approximately 190  Protein: 7g.   Fat: 8g.  Carbohydrates: 24g. Fiber: 6g.*

## Turkish Stuffed Eggplant (Imam Bayildi) Recipe

*Prep: 20min.        Cooking: 25min.        Serves: 4*

*Instructions:*

1. Prepare the Eggplants: Scoop out the center of each eggplant half to form a hollow, leaving a border around the skin.
2. Cook the Eggplant Flesh: Chop the scooped-out eggplant flesh. Mix it with onions, tomatoes, garlic, parsley, olive oil, cumin, paprika, salt, and pepper.
3. Preheat the Air Fryer: Set the air fryer to 180°C (350°F).
4. Cook the Eggplant Shells: Brush the eggplant halves with olive oil and air fry for 10 minutes, or until they start to soften.
5. Stuff the Eggplant: Fill the air-fried eggplant shells with the tomato and onion mixture.
6. Continue Cooking: Return the stuffed eggplants to the air fryer and cook for an additional 15 minutes, or until the filling is hot and the eggplants are tender.
7. Serve: Allow cooling slightly before serving, garnished with additional fresh parsley if desired.

*Ingredients:*

1. 2 large eggplants, halved lengthwise
2. 1 large onion, finely sliced
3. 2 tomatoes, diced
4. 4 cloves garlic, minced
5. 1/4 cup fresh parsley, chopped
6. 2 tablespoons olive oil, plus more for brushing
7. 1 teaspoon ground cumin
8. 1/2 teaspoon paprika
9. Salt and pepper to taste

*Calories: Approximately 200   Protein: 3g.   Fat: 10g.  Carbohydrates: 28g. Fiber: 11g.*

# Lunch

## Fennel and Orange Salad Recipe

*Prep: 15 min.      Cooking: 0min.      Serves: 4*

*Instructions:*

7. Prepare the Ingredients: Thinly slice the fennel bulbs segment the oranges. If using, slice the red onion and prepare the black olives and mint leaves.
8. Make the Dressing: Whisk together the olive oil, lemon juice, salt, and pepper to create the dressing.
9. Assemble the Salad: In a large bowl, combine the sliced fennel and orange segments. Drizzle with the dressing and toss gently to coat.
10. Serve: Arrange the salad on a serving platter and garnish with black olives, red onion slices, and fresh mint leaves if desired.

*Ingredients:*

1. 2 fennel bulbs, thinly sliced   and
2. 2 oranges, peeled and segmented
3. 1/4 cup olive oil
4. 2 tablespoons lemon juice
5. Salt and pepper to taste
6. Optional: black olives, red onion slices, and fresh mint leaves for garnish

*Calories: Approximately 200  Protein: 2g.   Fat: 14g.  Carbohydrates: 20g. Fiber: 5g.*

## Cauliflower Rice Recipe

*Prep: 10min.      Cooking: 15min.      Serves: 4*

*Instructions:*

1. Pulse the Cauliflower: In a food processor, pulse the cauliflower florets until they resemble rice grains.
2. Season: In a large bowl, mix the cauliflower rice with olive oil, garlic powder, oregano, paprika, salt, and pepper.
3. Preheat the Air Fryer: Set the air fryer to 200°C (390°F).
4. Cook: Spread the cauliflower rice in an even layer in the air fryer basket. Air fry for 15 minutes, stirring halfway through, until golden and slightly crispy.
5. Finish: Toss the cooked cauliflower rice with fresh parsley, lemon zest, and lemon juice. Add optional ingredients like diced tomatoes, olives, or feta cheese if desired.
6. Serve: Enjoy as a flavorful, low-carb side dish.

*Ingredients:*

1. 1 large head of cauliflower, cut into florets
2. 2 tablespoons olive oil
3. 1 teaspoon garlic powder
4. 1 teaspoon dried oregano
5. 1/2 teaspoon paprika
6. Salt and pepper to taste
7. 1/4 cup chopped fresh parsley
8. 1 lemon, zested and juiced
9. Optional: diced tomatoes, olives, or feta cheese for added flavor

*Calories: Approximately 100-150 (varies with added ingredients).*
*Protein: 3g.    Fat: 7g.   Carbohydrates: 10g.    Fiber: 11g.*

# Lunch

## Italian Mini Polenta Cakes Recipe

*Prep: 15 min.(plus cooling time for polenta)*     *Cooking: 15min.*     *Serves: 4*

### Instructions:

7. Prepare the Polenta: Mix the cooked polenta with grated Parmesan, basil, thyme, salt, and pepper until well combined. Let the polenta cool and set until firm enough to shape.
8. Form the Cakes: Once firm, shape the polenta mixture into small, round cakes, about the size of a cookie.
9. Preheat the Air Fryer: Set the air fryer to 200°C (390°F).
10. Cook the Cakes: Brush each polenta cake with olive oil and place them in the air fryer basket. Cook for 15 minutes, flipping halfway through, or until the cakes are golden and crispy on the outside.
11. Serve: Enjoy the mini polenta cakes hot as an appetizer or side dish, possibly with a dipping sauce or extra grated Parmesan.

### Ingredients:
1. 2 cups cooked polenta, cooled
2. 1/2 cup grated Parmesan cheese
3. 1 tablespoon fresh basil, chopped
4. 1 tablespoon fresh thyme, chopped
5. Salt and pepper to taste
6. Olive oil for brushing

*Calories: Approximately 200   Protein: 6g.   Fat: 8g.  Carbohydrates: 24g. Fiber: 2g.*

## Greek Fava Bean Dip with Air-Fried Pita Chips Recipe

*Prep: 10min.*     *Cooking: 10min.*     *Serves: 4*

### Instructions:

1. Make the Fava Bean Dip: Blend the fava beans, olive oil, lemon juice, garlic, salt, and pepper in a food processor until smooth and creamy. Adjust seasoning to taste.
2. Prepare the Pita Chips: Toss the pita triangles with olive oil, paprika (if using), and a pinch of salt.
3. Air Fry the Pita Chips: Preheat the air fryer to 180°C (350°F). Arrange the pita triangles in the air fryer basket in a single layer (you may need to do this in batches) and cook for about 5-10 minutes, or until golden and crispy.
4. Serve: Transfer the fava bean dip to a serving bowl, drizzle with a little extra olive oil, and garnish with chopped parsley or dill. Serve with the air-fried pita chips on the side.

### Ingredients:
**For the Fava Bean Dip:**
1. 2 cups cooked fava beans (or canned, drained and rinsed)
2. 1/4 cup olive oil, plus extra for serving
3. 1 lemon, juiced
4. 2 cloves garlic, minced
5. Salt and pepper to taste
6. Fresh parsley or dill, chopped for garnish

**For the Air-Fried Pita Chips:**
7. 4 pita bread rounds, cut into triangles
8. 2 tablespoons olive oil
9. 1/2 teaspoon paprika (optional)
10. Salt to taste

*Calories: Approximately 300   Protein: 10g.   Fat: 15g. Carbohydrates: 35g. Fiber: 8g.*

# Lunch

## Air-Fried Lamb Chops with Rosemary Recipe

*Prep: 10 min. (plus marinating time)*      *Cooking: 10-12min.*      *Serves: 4*

*Instructions:*

6. Marinate the Lamb Chops: Rub the lamb chops with olive oil, minced garlic, rosemary, salt, and pepper. them marinate for at least 30 minutes, or ideally a hours in the refrigerator.
7. Preheat the Air Fryer: Set the air fryer to 200°C (390°F).
8. Cook the Lamb Chops: Place the marinated lamb chops in the air fryer basket in a single layer. Air fry for 10-12 minutes, turning halfway through, or until they reach your desired level of doneness.
9. Rest and Serve: Let the lamb chops rest for a few minutes after cooking to allow the juices to redistribute. Serve hot, garnished with additional rosemary if desired.

*Ingredients:*
1. 4 lamb chops
2. 2 tablespoons olive oil
3. 2 cloves garlic, minced
4. 2 tablespoons fresh rosemary, chopped
5. Salt and pepper to taste

Let few

*Calories: Approximately 250   Protein: 20g.   Fat: 18g.   Carbohydrates: 0g. Fiber: 0g.*

## Tuna Patties Recipe

*Prep: 15min.*      *Cooking: 10min.*      *Serves: 4*

*Instructions:*

1. Prepare the Tuna Mixture: In a bowl, combine the drained tuna, breadcrumbs, eggs, parsley, lemon zest, lemon juice, garlic, salt, and pepper. Mix until well combined.
2. Form the Patties: Divide the mixture into eight equal portions and shape each into a patty.
3. Preheat the Air Fryer: Set the air fryer to 200°C (390°F).
4. Cook the Patties: Brush both sides of the patties with olive oil. Place them in the air fryer basket, ensuring they do not touch each other. Air fry for 10 minutes, flipping halfway through, or until golden and crispy on the outside.
5. Serve: Serve the tuna patties hot with a side of lemon wedges, tartar sauce, or a light salad.

*Ingredients:*
1. 2 cans (each 5 oz) tuna in water, drained
2. 1 cup breadcrumbs
3. 2 eggs
4. 1/4 cup fresh parsley, chopped
5. 1 lemon, zested and juiced
6. 2 cloves garlic, minced
7. Salt and pepper to taste
8. Olive oil for brushing

*Calories: Approximately 250   Protein: 25g.   Fat: 10g.   Carbohydrates: 15g.    Fiber: 1g.*

# Lunch

## Spanakorizo (Greek Spinach Rice) Recipe

*Prep: 10 min.      Cooking: 15min.      Serves: 4*

*Instructions:*

9. Sauté the Vegetables: In a skillet, heat one tablespoon of olive oil over medium heat. Add the onion and garlic, cooking until softened. Add the spinach and cook until wilted. Mix in the lemon juice, salt, and pepper.
10. Combine with Rice: Stir the cooked rice into the spinach mixture until well combined. If using, mix in the fresh dill or parsley.
11. Preheat the Air Fryer: Set the air fryer to 180°C (350°F).
12. Air-Fry the Mixture: Transfer the spinach and rice mixture to the air fryer basket. Drizzle with the remaining olive oil. Air fry for 15 minutes, stirring halfway through, until the rice gets a bit crispy on the edges.
13. Serve: Adjust the seasoning if needed and serve the Spanakorizo warm, with extra lemon wedges on the side if desired.

*Ingredients:*

1. 1 cup cooked rice, preferably a day old
2. 2 cups fresh spinach, chopped
3. 1 onion, finely chopped
4. 2 cloves garlic, minced
5. 2 tablespoons olive oil
6. 1/2 lemon, juiced
7. Salt and pepper to taste
8. Fresh dill or parsley, chopped (optional)

*Calories: Approximately 200   Protein: 4g.  Fat: 7g.  Carbohydrates: 30g. Fiber: 2g.*


## Roasted Red Pepper Hummus Recipe

*Prep: 10min. (excluding roasting time for the pepper)    Cooking: 15min. Serves: 4*

*Instructions:*

1. Roast the Red Pepper: Cut the red pepper into large pieces, removing the seeds. Preheat the air fryer to 200°C (390°F). Place the pepper pieces in the air fryer basket and cook for 15 minutes, or until the skin is charred and blistered. Remove and let cool, then peel off the skin.
2. Blend the Hummus: In a food processor, combine the roasted red pepper, chickpeas, tahini, garlic, olive oil, lemon juice, salt, pepper, and paprika if using. Blend until smooth and creamy.
3. Adjust the Seasoning: Taste and adjust the seasoning, adding more salt, pepper, or lemon juice if needed.
4. Serve: Transfer the hummus to a serving bowl. Drizzle with a little olive oil and sprinkle with paprika before serving with pita bread, vegetables, or air-fried pita chips.

*Ingredients:*

1. 1 can (15 oz) chickpeas, drained and rinsed
2. 1 large red bell pepper
3. 2 tablespoons tahini
4. 2 cloves garlic
5. 2 tablespoons olive oil
6. 1 lemon, juiced
7. Salt and pepper to taste
8. 1/2 teaspoon paprika (optional for smokiness)

*Calories: Approximately 200   Protein: 6g.  Fat: 12g.  Carbohydrates: 20g.   Fiber: 5g.*

# Lunch

## Air-Fried Cod with Olives and Tomatoes Recipe

*Prep: 10 min.      Cooking: 12min.      Serves: 4*

*Instructions:*

9. Prepare the Topping: In a bowl, mix the cherry tomatoes, olives, olive oil, garlic, oregano or thyme, and pepper.
10. Season the Cod: Lightly season the cod fillets with and pepper, and brush them with a bit of olive oil.
11. Preheat the Air Fryer: Set the air fryer to 180°C (350°F).
12. Cook the Cod: Place the cod fillets in the air fryer basket. Top each fillet with the tomato and olive mixture. Air fry for about 12 minutes, or until the cod cooked through and flakes easily with a fork.
13. Serve: Garnish the cod with fresh parsley or basil before serving.

*Ingredients:*

1. 4 cod fillets (about 6 ounces each)        salt,
2. 1 cup cherry tomatoes, halved
3. 1/2 cup olives, pitted and sliced        salt
4. 2 tablespoons olive oil
5. 1 clove garlic, minced
6. 1 teaspoon dried oregano or thyme
7. Salt and pepper to taste
8. Fresh parsley or basil, for garnish        is

*Calories: Approximately 200   Protein: 23g.   Fat: 10g.  Carbohydrates: 3g. Fiber: 1g.*

## Stuffed Artichokes with Garlic and Parmesan Recipe

*Prep: 20min.      Cooking: 20min.      Serves: 4*

*Instructions:*

1. Prepare the Artichokes: Trim the stems and top inches of the artichokes. Remove the center choke with a spoon. Boil or steam them until slightly tender but not fully cooked, about 10-15 minutes. Let cool.
2. Make the Filling: In a bowl, combine breadcrumbs, Parmesan cheese, minced garlic, parsley, salt, pepper, and olive oil to form a stuffing mixture.
3. Stuff the Artichokes: Gently spread the leaves of the cooled artichokes and spoon the garlic-Parmesan mixture into the spaces, filling them generously.
4. Preheat the Air Fryer: Set the air fryer to 180°C (350°F).
5. Cook the Artichokes: Place the stuffed artichokes in the air fryer basket. Drizzle with a little more olive oil. Air fry for 15-20 minutes, or until the tops are golden and crisp.
6. Serve: Allow the artichokes to cool slightly and serve with lemon wedges on the side.

*Ingredients:*

1. 4 large artichokes, trimmed and center choke removed
2. 1 cup breadcrumbs
3. 1/2 cup grated Parmesan cheese
4. 3 cloves garlic, minced
5. 1/4 cup fresh parsley, chopped
6. 1/4 cup olive oil, plus extra for drizzling
7. Salt and pepper to taste
8. Lemon wedges, for serving

*Calories: Approximately 300   Protein: 10g.   Fat: 18g.   Carbohydrates: 28g.    Fiber: 6g.*

# 50 Mediterranean dinner recipes

The collection of 50 Mediterranean dinner recipes showcases the diverse culinary traditions of the Mediterranean region, known for its healthy ingredients, bold flavors, and vibrant dishes. These recipes are designed to be prepared using an air fryer, offering a healthier cooking method that reduces oil usage while achieving delicious results.

Starting with Greek Chicken Gyros, we dive into the flavors of Greece with tender chicken, tangy tzatziki, and crisp cucumber salad wrapped in soft pita. Moving westward, we encounter Italian Air-Fried Ravioli, a crunchy outside with a succulent filling, and Spanish Patatas Bravas, where potatoes meet a spicy kick. From Lebanon, Falafel emerges as a beloved vegetarian delight, perfectly paired with tahini sauce.

The menu also explores the rich tastes of North Africa with Moroccan Spiced Eggplant, bringing together sweet, smoky, and spicy notes. The eastern Mediterranean is represented by Turkish Lamb Koftas and Israeli Shakshuka Bites, where traditional flavors are adapted to bite-sized delights. The list includes heartier meals like French Ratatouille and Italian Chicken Parmesan, demonstrating the Mediterranean's ability to merge simple ingredients into exquisite dishes.

Seafood plays a prominent role, with Spanish Air-Fried Cod with Romesco Sauce and Greek Air-Fried Octopus, showcasing the Mediterranean's love affair with the fruits of the sea. Vegetarian options abound, from Mediterranean Stuffed Bell Peppers to Lebanese Meatball Subs, highlighting the region's use of legumes and vegetables.

Innovative twists like Mediterranean Zucchini and Corn Fritters and Turkish Pumpkin and Lentil Soup reflect the adaptability of Mediterranean cuisine to modern tastes and cooking methods. Each recipe is thoughtfully crafted to bring out authentic flavors, whether it's the herbaceous punch of Greek Air-Fried Lamb Meatballs or the sweet and nutty profile of Moroccan Air-Fried Stuffed Dates.

Desserts and snacks are not forgotten, with Italian Air-Fried Polenta Cake and Greek Air-Fried Feta Cheese with Honey and Sesame offering a sweet or savory end to the meal. The collection also includes health-conscious choices like French Green Bean Almondine and Mediterranean Air-Fried Shrimp with Herbs and Garlic, ensuring options for every palate and dietary need.

To sum it up, this collection of 50 Mediterranean Air Fryer Dinner Recipes is a celebration of the region's culinary diversity, combining traditional and modern flavors to create dishes that are flavorful, nutritious, and easy to prepare. Each recipe promises a delightful dining experience, echoing the Mediterranean's sunny skies and rich landscapes.

# Dinner

## Greek Chicken Gyros with Tzatziki and Cucumber Salad in Pita

*Prep: 20 min.(plus marinating time)*     *Cooking: 15min.*     *Serves: 4*

*Instructions:*

1. Marinate the Chicken: Mix olive oil, oregano, garlic, lemon juice, salt, and pepper in a bowl. Add chicken and marinate for at least 30 minutes, preferably a few hours.
2. Make the Tzatziki: Combine Greek yogurt, grated cucumber, garlic, dill, lemon juice, salt, and pepper in a bowl. Chill until ready to serve.
3. Prepare the Cucumber Salad: Toss sliced cucumber, red onion, and tomatoes with olive oil, lemon juice, salt, and pepper.
4. Preheat the Air Fryer: Set the air fryer to 200°C (390°F).
5. Cook the Chicken: Place marinated chicken in the air fryer basket and cook for 15 minutes, turning halfway through, or until fully cooked and golden brown.
6. Assemble the Gyros: Warm the pita bread in the air fryer or on a skillet. Slice the chicken into strips. On each pita, place chicken, tzatziki, and cucumber salad. Fold and serve.

*Calories: Approximately 500-600*     *Protein: 40g.*     *Fat: 20g.*
*Carbohydrates: 50g.*     *Fiber: 3g.*

*Ingredients:*
1. 4 boneless, skinless chicken thighs or breasts
2. 2 tablespoons olive oil
3. 1 tablespoon dried oregano
4. 2 cloves garlic, minced
5. Juice of 1 lemon
6. Salt and pepper to taste
7. 4 pita bread rounds
8. For the Tzatziki:
9. 1 cup Greek yogurt
10. 1 cucumber, grated and excess water squeezed out
11. 2 cloves garlic, minced
12. 2 tablespoons fresh dill, chopped
13. Juice of 1/2 lemon
14. Salt and pepper to taste
15. For the Cucumber Salad:
16. 1 cucumber, sliced
17. 1/4 red onion, thinly sliced
18. 2 tomatoes, sliced
19. Olive oil, lemon juice, salt, and pepper for dressing

## Italian Air-Fried Ravioli with Marinara Dipping Sauce

*Prep: 15min.*     *Cooking: 10min.*     *Serves: 4*

*Instructions:*

1. Prep the Ravioli: Thaw the ravioli if frozen. Combine breadcrumbs, Parmesan cheese, Italian seasoning, salt, and pepper in a bowl. Dip each ravioli in the beaten eggs, then coat with the breadcrumb mixture.
2. Preheat the Air Fryer: Set the air fryer to 200°C (400°F).
3. Air-Fry the Ravioli: Spray the air fryer basket with olive oil. Place the coated ravioli in a single layer in the basket (cook in batches if needed) and spray the tops with olive oil. Air fry for about 8-10 minutes, flipping halfway through, until golden brown and crispy.
4. Heat the Marinara Sauce: While the ravioli are cooking, warm the marinara sauce in a saucepan or in the microwave.
5. Serve: Serve the hot, crispy ravioli with the warm marinara sauce for dipping.

*Ingredients:*
1. 1 package (about 16 oz) of fresh or frozen ravioli
2. 1 cup breadcrumbs
3. 1/2 cup grated Parmesan cheese
4. 2 eggs, beaten
5. 1 teaspoon Italian seasoning
6. Salt and pepper to taste
7. Olive oil spray
8. 1 cup marinara sauce, for dipping

*Calories: Approximately 350-400*     *Protein: 16g.*     *Fat: 15g.*     *Carbohydrates: 40g.*     *Fiber: 3g.*

# Dinner

## Moroccan Spiced Eggplant with Harissa and Yogurt

*Prep: 10 min.        Cooking: 15min.        Serves: 4*

*Instructions:*

1. Season the Eggplant: Mix the olive oil, harissa paste, cumin, smoked paprika, salt, and pepper in a bowl. Brush both sides of the eggplant slices with this mixture.
2. Preheat the Air Fryer: Set the air fryer to 200°C (390°F).
3. Air-Fry the Eggplant: Place the seasoned eggplant slices in the air fryer basket in a single layer. Cook for 15 minutes, turning halfway through, until tender and slightly charred.
4. Prepare the Yogurt Sauce: While the eggplant is cooking, mix the Greek yogurt, minced garlic, lemon juice, and a pinch of salt in a bowl.
5. Serve: Place the cooked eggplant on a serving platter, drizzle with the yogurt sauce, and garnish with chopped cilantro or parsley.

*Ingredients:*

1. 2 large eggplants, sliced into 1/2-inch rounds
2. 2 tablespoons olive oil
3. 2 tablespoons harissa paste
4. 1 teaspoon ground cumin
5. 1 teaspoon smoked paprika
6. Salt and pepper to taste
7. 1 cup Greek yogurt
8. 1 clove garlic, minced
9. 1 tablespoon lemon juice
10. Fresh cilantro or parsley, chopped for garnish

*Calories: Approximately 200    Protein: 6g.    Fat: 10g.    Carbohydrates: 25g.    Fiber: 9g.*

## Spanish Patatas Bravas with Spicy Aioli

*Prep: 10min.        Cooking: 20min.        Serves: 4*

*Instructions:*

1. Prepare the Potatoes: Toss the cubed potatoes with olive oil, smoked paprika, salt, and pepper.
2. Preheat the Air Fryer: Set the air fryer to 200°C (400°F).
3. Cook the Potatoes: Place the seasoned potatoes in the air fryer basket in a single layer. Air fry for 20 minutes, shaking halfway through, until they are golden and crispy.
4. Make the Spicy Aioli: While the potatoes are cooking, mix mayonnaise, minced garlic, lemon juice, hot sauce, and salt in a small bowl to create the aioli.
5. Serve: Serve the crispy potatoes hot, drizzled with or dipped into the spicy aioli.
6. Serve: Serve the hot, crispy ravioli with the warm marinara sauce for dipping.

*Ingredients:*

1. 4 large potatoes, peeled and cubed
2. 2 tablespoons olive oil
3. 1 teaspoon smoked paprika
4. 1/2 teaspoon salt
5. 1/4 teaspoon ground black pepper

*For the Spicy Aioli:*

6. 1/2 cup mayonnaise
7. 1 garlic clove, minced
8. 1 tablespoon lemon juice
9. 1-2 teaspoons hot sauce or to taste
10. Salt to taste

*Calories: Approximately 300    Protein: 4g.    Fat: 16g.    Carbohydrates: 35g.    Fiber: 4g.*

# Dinner

## Lebanese Falafel with Tahini Sauce

*Prep: 30 min.(plus soaking time).*     *Cooking: 20min.*     *Serves: 4*

*Instructions:*
1. Prepare the Falafel Mixture: Drain the soaked chickpeas and combine them in a food processor with onion, garlic, parsley, cumin, coriander, cayenne, salt, and pepper. Process until mixture is finely ground. Transfer to a bowl, stir in baking powder and flour, and let it rest for 15 minutes.
2. Form the Falafel: Shape the mixture into small balls or patties.
3. Preheat the Air Fryer: Set the air fryer to 190°C (375°F).
4. Cook the Falafel: Place the falafel in the air fryer basket in a single layer, spraying lightly with oil. Air fry for 10 minutes, flip, and cook for another 10 minutes until golden and crispy.
5. Make the Tahini Sauce: Whisk together tahini, lemon juice, garlic, and salt. Add water until the sauce reaches desired consistency.
6. Serve: Serve the falafel hot with tahini sauce on the side for dipping.

*Calories: Approximately 330*    *Protein: 13g.*    *Fat: 15g.*
*Carbohydrates: 40g.*    *Fiber: 9g.*

*Ingredients:*
*For the Falafel:*
1. 2 cups dried chickpeas, soaked overnight (do not use canned chickpeas)
2. 1 small onion, chopped
3. 2 cloves of garlic, minced
4. 1/4 cup fresh parsley, chopped
5. 2 teaspoons ground cumin
6. 1 teaspoon ground coriander
7. 1/2 teaspoon cayenne pepper (adjust to taste)
8. Salt and pepper to taste
9. 1 teaspoon baking powder
10. 2 tablespoons all-purpose flour (or chickpea flour for gluten-free)

*For the Tahini Sauce:*
11. 1/2 cup tahini
12. 1/4 cup lemon juice
13. 1 clove garlic, minced
14. Salt to taste
15. Water, as needed to thin the sauce

## French Ratatouille with Thyme and Basil

*Prep: 15min.*     *Cooking: 20min.*     *Serves: 4*

*Instructions:*
2. Prepare the Vegetables: In a large bowl, toss the eggplant, zucchinis, bell pepper, tomatoes, onion, and garlic with olive oil, thyme, basil, salt, and pepper.
3. Preheat the Air Fryer: Set the air fryer to 180°C (350°F).
4. Cook the Ratatouille: Place the vegetable mixture in the air fryer basket. Cook for 20 minutes, stirring halfway through, until the vegetables are tender and lightly browned.
5. Serve: Check for seasoning, adjust if necessary, and serve the ratatouille warm as a side dish or a light main course.

*Ingredients:*
1 small eggplant, cubed
2 zucchinis, cubed
1 bell pepper, cubed
2 tomatoes, chopped
1 onion, chopped
3 cloves garlic, minced
2 tablespoons olive oil
1 teaspoon fresh thyme, chopped
1 teaspoon fresh basil, chopped
1. Salt and pepper to taste

*Calories: Approximately 150*    *Protein: 3g.*    *Fat: 7g.*    *Carbohydrates: 20g.*    *Fiber: 6g.*

# Dinner

## Turkish Lamb Koftas with Mint Yogurt Dip

*Prep: 20min.        Cooking: 15min.        Serves: 4*

*Instructions:*

1. Make the Kofta Mixture: In a bowl, combine ground lamb, grated onion, minced garlic, parsley, cumin, paprika, coriander, salt, and pepper. Mix well.
2. Form the Koftas: Shape the mixture into elongated meatballs or sausage shapes.
3. Preheat the Air Fryer: Set the air fryer to 200°C (390°F).
4. Cook the Koftas: Place the koftas in the air fryer basket, ensuring they are not touching. Cook for 15 minutes, turning halfway through, until browned and cooked through.
5. Prepare the Mint Yogurt Dip: While the koftas are cooking, combine Greek yogurt, mint, minced garlic, lemon juice, and salt in a bowl.
6. Serve: Serve the hot koftas with the mint yogurt dip on the side.

*Ingredients:*
*For the Koftas:*
1. 500g ground lamb
2. 1 onion, finely grated
3. 2 cloves garlic, minced
4. 2 tablespoons fresh parsley, chopped
5. 1 teaspoon ground cumin
6. 1 teaspoon paprika
7. 1/2 teaspoon ground coriander
8. Salt and pepper to taste

*For the Mint Yogurt Dip:*
9. 1 cup Greek yogurt
10. 2 tablespoons fresh mint, chopped
11. 1 clove garlic, minced
12. 1 tablespoon lemon juice
13. Salt to tasteSalt to taste

*Calories: Approximately 400   Protein: 25g.   Fat: 30g.   Carbohydrates: 5g.     Fiber: 1g.*


## Greek Spanakopita Bites with Spinach and Feta

*Prep: 20min.        Cooking: 15min.        Serves: 4-6*

*Instructions:*

1. Prepare the Filling: In a bowl, combine the spinach, feta cheese, ricotta (if using), onion, garlic, dill, salt, and pepper. Mix well.
2. Assemble the Bites: Cut the phyllo dough into squares (about 4x4 inches). Brush each square with olive oil or melted butter. Place a small spoonful of the spinach and feta mixture in the center of each square. Fold the corners of the phyllo over the filling to form a bite-sized parcel.
3. Preheat the Air Fryer: Set the air fryer to 180°C (350°F).
4. Cook the Spanakopita Bites: Place the spanakopita bites in the air fryer basket in a single layer, ensuring they don't touch. Air fry for 12-15 minutes, or until golden brown and crispy.
5. Serve: Serve warm, ideal for a savory snack or appetizer.

*Ingredients:*
1. 1 package frozen spinach, thawed and squeezed dry
2. 1 cup feta cheese, crumbled
3. 1/2 cup ricotta cheese (optional, for creaminess)
4. 1 small onion, finely chopped
5. 2 cloves garlic, minced
6. 2 tablespoons fresh dill, chopped
7. Salt and pepper to taste
8. 1 package phyllo dough, thawed
9. 1/4 cup olive oil or melted butter for brushing

*Calories: Approximately 300   Protein: 10g.   Fat: 20g.   Carbohydrates: 20g.     Fiber: 2g.*

# Dinner

## Egyptian Taameya (Fava Bean Falafel) with Garlic Lemon Sauce

*Prep: 20min. (plus soaking time)*     *Cooking: 20min.*     *Serves: 4*

*Instructions:*

1. Prepare the Taameya Mixture: Drain the soaked fava beans and blend them in a food processor with onion, garlic, parsley, cilantro, cumin, coriander, salt, and pepper until smooth. Stir in baking powder just before cooking.
2. Form the Taameya Balls: Shape the mixture into small balls or patties.
3. Preheat the Air Fryer: Set the air fryer to 180°C (350°F).
4. Cook the Taameya: Place the balls in the air fryer basket in a single layer, and cook for 10 minutes, flip, and continue cooking for another 10 minutes until golden and crispy.
5. Make the Garlic Lemon Sauce: While the taameya is cooking, mix olive oil, minced garlic, lemon juice, and salt in a small bowl.
6. Serve: Serve the taameya hot with the garlic lemon sauce on the side for dipping.

*Ingredients:*
*For the Taameya:*

1. 2 cups dried split fava beans, soaked overnight
2. 1 small onion, chopped
3. 2 cloves garlic, minced
4. 1/2 cup fresh parsley, chopped
5. 1/2 cup fresh cilantro, chopped
6. 1 teaspoon ground cumin
7. 1 teaspoon ground coriander
8. Salt and pepper to taste
9. 1 teaspoon baking powder

*For the Garlic Lemon Sauce:*

10. 1/4 cup olive oil
11. 3 cloves garlic, minced
12. 2 tablespoons lemon juice
13. Salt to taste

*Calories: Approximately 300   Protein: 12g.   Fat: 15g.   Carbohydrates: 30g.   Fiber: 9g.*

## Italian Caprese Stuffed Portobello Mushrooms

*Prep: 10min.*     *Cooking: 10min.*     *Serves: 4*

*Instructions:*

1. Prepare the Mushrooms: Clean the mushrooms and remove the stems. Brush both sides of the caps with olive oil and season with salt and pepper.
2. Preheat the Air Fryer: Set the air fryer to 200°C (390°F).
3. Stuff the Mushrooms: Place the mushroom caps, gill-side up, in the air fryer basket. Fill each cap with tomato halves and slices of mozzarella cheese.
4. Cook the Mushrooms: Air fry for 10 minutes, or until the cheese is melted and bubbly, and the mushrooms are tender.
5. Serve: Top the stuffed mushrooms with fresh basil leaves and drizzle with balsamic glaze before serving.

*Ingredients:*

1. 4 large Portobello mushrooms, stems removed
2. 2 tablespoons olive oil
3. Salt and pepper to taste
4. 1 cup cherry tomatoes, halved
5. 1 ball fresh mozzarella cheese, sliced
6. Fresh basil leaves
7. Balsamic glaze for drizzling

*Calories: Approximately 200   Protein: 10g.   Fat: 15g.   Carbohydrates: 8g.   Fiber: 2g.*

# Dinner

## Israeli Shakshuka Bites with Poached Eggs and Tomato Sauce

*Prep: 15min.      Cooking: 20min.      Serves: 4*

*Instructions:*

1. Prepare the Shakshuka Sauce: In a pan, sauté the onion, bell pepper, and garlic with olive oil until softened. Add the tomato sauce, season with salt, pepper, cumin, paprika, and chili, and cook until the sauce thickens slightly.
2. Preheat the Air Fryer: Set the air fryer to 180°C (350°F).
3. Assemble the Bites: Spoon the sauce into small, oven-safe ramekins or silicone molds that can fit in the air fryer. Make a well in the center of each and carefully crack an egg into each well.
4. Cook in the Air Fryer: Place the ramekins in the air fryer basket. Air fry for about 10-12 minutes, or until the egg whites are set but yolks are still runny.
5. Serve: Carefully remove the ramekins and serve the shakshuka bites immediately, garnished with fresh herbs if desired.

*Ingredients:*
*For the Shakshuka Bites:*
1. 1 cup tomato sauce (preferably spiced with cumin, paprika, and chili)
2. 1 bell pepper, finely diced
3. 1 small onion, finely diced
4. 2 cloves garlic, minced
5. Olive oil
6. Salt and pepper to taste

*For the Poached Eggs:*
7. 4 eggs
8. Vinegar (to help set the egg whites)

*Calories: Approximately 200   Protein: 10g.   Fat: 12g.   Carbohydrates: 10g.     Fiber: 2g.*

## Spanish Chorizo and White Bean Stew

*Prep: 10min.      Cooking: 20min.      Serves: 4*

*Instructions:*

1. Sauté the Chorizo and Vegetables: In a skillet or on the stove, heat olive oil over medium heat. Add the chorizo, onion, garlic, and bell pepper. Sauté until the onion is translucent and chorizo is slightly browned.
2. Preheat the Air Fryer: If using the air fryer to finish the stew, preheat it to 150°C (300°F).
3. Combine Ingredients: Transfer the sautéed mixture to an air fryer-safe dish or continue in the skillet if finishing on the stove. Add the white beans, diced tomatoes, smoked paprika, cayenne pepper, and broth. Stir to combine.
4. Cook the Stew: If using the air fryer, place the dish in the basket and cook for 20 minutes, stirring halfway through. On the stove, simmer the stew for about 20 minutes until the flavors meld and the stew thickens.
5. Serve: Season with salt and pepper to taste. Garnish with fresh parsley and serve hot.

*Ingredients:*
1. 200g chorizo, sliced
2. 1 can (15 oz) white beans, drained and rinsed
3. 1 onion, chopped
4. 2 cloves garlic, minced
5. 1 bell pepper, chopped
6. 1 can (14 oz) diced tomatoes
7. 1 teaspoon smoked paprika
8. 1/2 teaspoon cayenne pepper (optional, for heat)
9. 2 cups chicken or vegetable broth
10. Salt and pepper to taste
11. 2 tablespoons olive oil
12. Fresh parsley, chopped for garnish

*Calories: Approximately 350   Protein: 18g.   Fat: 20g.   Carbohydrates: 25g.     Fiber: 6g.*

# Dinner

## Stuffed Bell Peppers with Quinoa and Herbs

*Prep: 20min.*     *Cooking: 20min.*     *Serves: 4*

*Instructions:*

1. Prepare the Filling: In a bowl, mix the cooked quinoa, onion, garlic, tomato, feta cheese, olives, parsley, mint, olive oil, salt, and pepper.
2. Stuff the Peppers: Spoon the quinoa mixture into each bell pepper, filling them up evenly.
3. Preheat the Air Fryer: Set the air fryer to 180°C (350°F).
4. Cook the Peppers: Place the stuffed peppers in the air fryer basket. Cook for 20 minutes, or until the peppers are tender and the filling is heated through.
5. Serve: Let the peppers cool slightly before serving. They can be garnished with additional herbs or a drizzle of olive oil if desired.

*Ingredients:*

1. 4 large bell peppers, tops cut off and seeds removed
2. 1 cup quinoa, cooked
3. 1 onion, finely chopped
4. 2 cloves garlic, minced
5. 1 tomato, diced
6. 1/2 cup feta cheese, crumbled
7. 1/4 cup olives, chopped
8. 1/4 cup fresh parsley, chopped
9. 1/4 cup fresh mint, chopped
10. 2 tablespoons olive oil
11. Salt and pepper to taste

*Calories: Approximately 300*   *Protein: 10g.*   *Fat: 15g.*   *Carbohydrates: 35g.*   *Fiber: 6g.*

## Italian Chicken Parmesan

*Prep: 15min.*     *Cooking: 20min.*     *Serves: 4*

*Instructions:*

1. Prepare the Chicken: Pound the chicken breasts to an even thickness. Season with salt and pepper.
2. Bread the Chicken: Mix breadcrumbs, Parmesan cheese, Italian seasoning, and garlic powder in a shallow dish. Dip each chicken breast in the beaten eggs, then coat with the breadcrumb mixture.
3. Preheat the Air Fryer: Set the air fryer to 180°C (350°F).
4. Cook the Chicken: Brush the air fryer basket with olive oil. Place the breaded chicken in the basket and cook for 10 minutes. Flip the chicken, top each breast with marinara sauce and mozzarella cheese, and cook for another 10 minutes, or until the chicken is cooked through and the cheese is melted and bubbly.
5. Serve: Garnish with fresh basil and serve hot.

*Ingredients:*

1. 4 boneless, skinless chicken breasts
2. 1 cup breadcrumbs
3. 1/2 cup grated Parmesan cheese
4. 1 teaspoon Italian seasoning
5. 1/2 teaspoon garlic powder
6. Salt and pepper to taste
7. 2 eggs, beaten
8. 1 cup marinara sauce
9. 1 cup shredded mozzarella cheese
10. 2 tablespoons olive oil
11. Fresh basil for garnish

*Calories: Approximately 400*   *Protein: 38g.*   *Fat: 18g.*   *Carbohydrates: 20g.*   *Fiber: 1g.*

# Dinner

## Greek Lemon Roasted Potatoes

*Prep: 10min.        Cooking: 25min.        Serves: 4*

*Instructions:*

1. Prepare the Potatoes: In a large bowl, toss the potato wedges with olive oil, lemon juice, minced garlic, oregano, salt, and pepper.
2. Preheat the Air Fryer: Set the air fryer to 200°C (400°F).
3. Cook the Potatoes: Arrange the potato wedges in the air fryer basket. Pour the broth over the potatoes. Air fry for 25 minutes, or until the potatoes are golden brown and crispy, shaking the basket halfway through the cooking time.
4. Serve: Remove the potatoes from the air fryer and let them rest for a few minutes before serving. They should be crispy on the outside and tender on the inside.
5. Nutritional Value (per serving)

*Calories: Approximately 300   Protein: 6g.   Fat: 14g.   Carbohydrates: 40g.     Fiber: 5g.*

*Ingredients:*

1. 6 large potatoes, peeled and cut into wedges
2. 1/4 cup olive oil
3. Juice of 2 lemons
4. 2 cloves garlic, minced
5. 2 teaspoons dried oregano
6. Salt and pepper to taste
7. 1/2 cup chicken or vegetable broth

## Moroccan Chicken Tagine with Olives and Lemon

*Prep: 15min.        Cooking: 25min.        Serves: 4*

*Instructions:*

1. Season the Chicken: Rub the chicken thighs with salt, pepper, cumin, coriander, cinnamon, and turmeric.
2. Preheat the Air Fryer: Set the air fryer to 180°C (350°F).
3. Brown the Chicken: In a skillet, heat olive oil over medium heat. Add the chicken and brown on both sides. Transfer to a plate.
4. Sauté the Vegetables: In the same skillet, add the onion and garlic, cooking until softened.
5. Combine in the Air Fryer: Place the browned chicken, sautéed onion and garlic, chicken broth, preserved lemon, and olives in an air fryer-safe dish or pot that fits in the air fryer basket.
6. Cook the Tagine: Air fry for 20-25 minutes, or until the chicken is cooked through and tender.
7. Serve: Garnish with fresh cilantro or parsley and serve hot, ideally with couscous or bread.

*Calories: Approximately 350   Protein: 25g.   Fat: 25g.
Carbohydrates: 10g.     Fiber: 2g.*

*Ingredients:*

1. 4 chicken thighs, bone-in and skin-on
2. 2 tablespoons olive oil
3. 1 onion, chopped
4. 2 cloves garlic, minced
5. 1 teaspoon ground cumin
6. 1 teaspoon ground coriander
7. 1/2 teaspoon ground cinnamon
8. 1/2 teaspoon turmeric
9. Salt and pepper to taste
10. 1 cup chicken broth
11. 1 lemon, preserved and sliced
12. 1/2 cup green olives
13. Fresh cilantro or parsley, for garnish

# Dinner

## Sicilian Cauliflower Steaks with Capers and Raisins

*Prep: 10min.     Cooking: 15min.     Serves: 4*

*Instructions:*

1. Prepare the Cauliflower: Brush the cauliflower steaks with olive oil and season with salt and pepper.
2. Preheat the Air Fryer: Set the air fryer to 200°C (390°F).
3. Cook the Cauliflower Steaks: Place the cauliflower steaks in the air fryer basket in a single layer. Cook for 15 minutes, turning halfway through, until they are golden brown and tender.
4. Prepare the Topping: While the cauliflower cooks, combine capers, raisins, minced garlic, and red wine vinegar in a small bowl. Set aside to let the flavors meld.
5. Serve: Place the cooked cauliflower steaks on a serving platter, spoon the caper and raisin mixture over the steaks, garnish with fresh parsley, and serve immediately.

*Ingredients:*
1. 1 large head of cauliflower, sliced into 1-inch thick steaks
2. 3 tablespoons olive oil
3. Salt and pepper to taste
4. 2 tablespoons capers, rinsed
5. 2 tablespoons raisins
6. 1 garlic clove, minced
7. 1 tablespoon red wine vinegar
8. Fresh parsley, chopped for garnish

*Calories: Approximately 150   Protein: 4g.   Fat: 10g.   Carbohydrates: 14g.    Fiber: 3g.*


## Spanish Air-Fried Cod with Romesco Sauce

*Prep: 15min.     Cooking: 12min.     Serves: 4*

*Instructions:*

1. Prepare the Cod: Season the cod fillets with salt, pepper, and smoked paprika. Drizzle with olive oil.
2. Preheat the Air Fryer: Set the air fryer to 180°C (350°F).
3. Cook the Cod: Place the cod fillets in the air fryer basket. Air fry for 12 minutes or until the fish is cooked through and flakes easily with a fork.
4. Make the Romesco Sauce: While the cod is cooking, blend the roasted red pepper, almonds, tomato, garlic, olive oil, red wine vinegar, smoked paprika, salt, and pepper in a food processor until smooth.
5. Serve: Plate the cooked cod and spoon the Romesco sauce over the fillets. Serve immediately.

*Ingredients:*
*For the Cod:*
1. 4 cod fillets (about 6 ounces each)
2. 2 tablespoons olive oil
3. Salt and pepper to taste
4. 1 teaspoon smoked paprika

*For the Romesco Sauce:*
5. 1 roasted red bell pepper, peeled and deseeded
6. 1/4 cup almonds, toasted
7. 1 tomato, chopped
8. 1 garlic clove
9. 2 tablespoons olive oil
10. 1 tablespoon red wine vinegar
11. 1 teaspoon smoked paprika
12. Salt and pepper to taste

*Calories: Approximately 300   Protein: 25g.   Fat: 18g.*
*Carbohydrates: 8g.    Fiber: 2g.*

# Dinner

## Turkish Stuffed Eggplants (Imam Bayildi)

*Prep: 20min.          Cooking: 25min.          Serves: 4*

*Instructions:*

1. Prepare the Eggplants: Slice the eggplants in half lengthwise and scoop out some of the flesh to create a boat shape. Chop the scooped-out flesh and set aside.
2. Sauté the Filling: Heat olive oil in a pan and sauté the onion, garlic, and chopped eggplant until softened. Add the tomatoes, parsley, cumin, paprika, salt, and pepper, and cook until the mixture is tender.
3. Stuff the Eggplants: Fill the eggplant halves with the vegetable mixture.
4. Preheat the Air Fryer: Set the air fryer to 180°C (350°F).
5. Cook the Eggplants: Place the stuffed eggplants in the air fryer basket. Add water or broth to the bottom of the basket to prevent drying out. Air fry for 25 minutes, or until the eggplants are tender and the tops are slightly browned.
6. Serve: Let the Imam Bayildi cool for a few minutes before serving. It can be garnished with additional fresh parsley if desired.

*Ingredients:*
1. 4 medium eggplants
2. 1 onion, finely chopped
3. 4 cloves garlic, minced
4. 2 tomatoes, diced
5. 1/4 cup fresh parsley, chopped
6. 1/4 cup olive oil, plus extra for brushing
7. 1 teaspoon ground cumin
8. 1/2 teaspoon paprika
9. Salt and pepper to taste
10. 1/2 cup water or vegetable broth

*Calories: Approximately 250   Protein: 4g.   Fat: 18g.   Carbohydrates: 20g.   Fiber: 8g.*

## Lebanese Meatball Subs with Pine Nuts and Tomato Sauce

*Prep: 20min.          Cooking: 20min.          Serves: 4*

*Instructions:*

1. Prepare the Meatballs: In a bowl, combine ground meat, pine nuts, onion, garlic, parsley, cumin, allspice, salt, and pepper. Form into small meatballs.
2. Preheat the Air Fryer: Set the air fryer to 180°C (350°F).
3. Cook the Meatballs: Place meatballs in the air fryer basket and cook for 10 minutes, turning halfway through, until browned and cooked through.
4. Prepare the Tomato Sauce: Simmer the tomato sauce in a pan with dried mint, salt, and pepper until heated through.
5. Assemble the Subs: Slice the sub rolls open, fill with meatballs, top with tomato sauce, and sprinkle with cheese if using.
6. Melt the Cheese: Place the subs back in the air fryer for 2-3 minutes, or until the cheese is melted and the bread is toasted.
7. Serve: Serve the subs hot, garnished with additional parsley or mint if desired.

*Ingredients:*
*For the Meatballs:*
1. 500g ground beef or lamb
2. 1/4 cup pine nuts, toasted
3. 1 small onion, finely chopped
4. 2 cloves garlic, minced
5. 1/4 cup fresh parsley, chopped
6. 1 teaspoon ground cumin
7. 1/2 teaspoon ground allspice
8. Salt and pepper to taste

*For the Tomato Sauce:*
9. 2 cups tomato sauce
10. 1 teaspoon dried mint
11. Salt and pepper to taste

*To Assemble:*
12. 4 sub rolls or baguettes
13. 1 cup shredded mozzarella or provolone cheese (optional)

*Calories: Approximately 600-700   Protein: 35g.   Fat: 30g.   Carbohydrates: 50g.   Fiber: 5g.*

# Dinner

## Greek Pita Pizzas with Olives and Feta

*Prep: 10min.*      *Cooking: 8min.*      *Serves: 4*

*Instructions:*

1. Prepare the Pita Pizzas: Spread tomato sauce evenly over each pita bread. Top with feta cheese, Kalamata olives, sliced onion, and bell pepper. Sprinkle with dried oregano.
2. Preheat the Air Fryer: Set the air fryer to 200°C (390°F).
3. Cook the Pita Pizzas: Place the prepared pitas in the air fryer basket (cook in batches if necessary) and cook for 6-8 minutes or until the edges are crispy and the cheese is melted and slightly golden.
4. Serve: Drizzle with olive oil and garnish with fresh basil or parsley before serving.

*Ingredients:*
1. 4 pita bread rounds
2. 1 cup tomato sauce
3. 1 cup feta cheese, crumbled
4. 1/2 cup Kalamata olives, pitted and sliced
5. 1 red onion, thinly sliced
6. 1 bell pepper, thinly sliced
7. 1 teaspoon dried oregano
8. Olive oil for drizzling
9. Fresh basil or parsley for garnish

*Calories: Approximately 350   Protein: 12g.   Fat: 18g.   Carbohydrates: 36g.    Fiber: 3g.*

## Italian Prosciutto Wrapped Asparagus

*Prep: 10min.*      *Cooking: 8min.*      *Serves: 4*

*Instructions:*

1. Prepare the Asparagus: Lightly coat the asparagus spears with olive oil and season with black pepper.
2. Wrap with Prosciutto: Wrap each asparagus spear with a strip of prosciutto, covering most of the spear.
3. Preheat the Air Fryer: Set the air fryer to 200°C (400°F).
4. Cook the Asparagus: Place the wrapped asparagus in the air fryer basket in a single layer. Air fry for 6-8 minutes, or until the asparagus is tender and the prosciutto is crispy.
5. Serve: Garnish with Parmesan shavings if desired and serve with lemon wedges on the side.

*Ingredients:*
1. 16 asparagus spears, trimmed
2. 8 slices of prosciutto, halved lengthwise
3. 1 tablespoon olive oil
4. Black pepper to taste
5. Parmesan cheese shavings, for garnish (optional)
6. Lemon wedges, for serving

*Calories: Approximately 600-700   Protein: 35g.   Fat: 30g.   Carbohydrates: 50g.    Fiber: 5g.*

# Dinner

## Moroccan Carrot Salad with Cumin and Mint

*Prep: 15min.        Cooking: 15min.        Serves: 4*

*Instructions:*

1. Season the Carrots: Toss the carrot slices with olive oil, cumin, salt, and pepper.
2. Preheat the Air Fryer: Set the air fryer to 180°C (350°F).
3. Cook the Carrots: Arrange the seasoned carrots in the air fryer basket in a single layer. Air fry for 15 minutes, or until tender and slightly caramelized, shaking the basket halfway through.
4. Prepare the Salad: In a large bowl, combine the cooked carrots, chopped mint, lemon juice, honey (if using), raisins, and toasted almonds.
5. Serve: Toss the salad ingredients together and serve either warm or at room temperature.

*Ingredients:*
1. 500g carrots, peeled and sliced into thin rounds
2. 2 tablespoons olive oil
3. 1 teaspoon ground cumin
4. Salt and pepper to taste
5. 2 tablespoons fresh mint, chopped
6. 1 tablespoon lemon juice
7. 1 teaspoon honey (optional)
8. 1/4 cup raisins or dried cranberries
9. 1/4 cup slivered almonds, toasted

*Calories: Approximately 200    Protein: 3g.   Fat: 10g.   Carbohydrates: 28g.    Fiber: 6g.*


## Cypriot Halloumi Fries

*Prep: 5min.       Cooking: 10min.        Serves: 4*

*Instructions:*

1. Prepare the Halloumi: Toss the halloumi fries with olive oil and paprika or za'atar seasoning until evenly coated.
2. Preheat the Air Fryer: Set the air fryer to 200°C (390°F).
3. Cook the Halloumi Fries: Arrange the seasoned halloumi fries in the air fryer basket in a single layer. Air fry for 10 minutes, turning halfway through, until golden brown and crispy on the outside.
4. Serve: Serve the halloumi fries hot, garnished with fresh mint or parsley, and accompanied by lemon wedges and optional dipping sauces.

*Ingredients:*
1. 250g halloumi cheese, cut into thick fries
2. 1 tablespoon olive oil
3. 1 teaspoon paprika or za'atar seasoning
4. Lemon wedges, for serving
5. Fresh mint or parsley, chopped, for garnish
6. Optional dipping sauces: tzatziki or harissa

*Calories: Approximately 200    Protein: 14g.   Fat: 15g.   Carbohydrates: 2g.    Fiber: 0g.*

# Dinner

## Spanish Garlic Shrimp (Gambas al Ajillo)

*Prep: 10min.        Cooking: 8min.        Serves: 4*

*Instructions:*

1. Marinate the Shrimp: In a bowl, combine shrimp, olive oil, garlic, red pepper flakes, smoked paprika, and salt. Let it marinate for about 10 minutes.
2. Preheat the Air Fryer: Set the air fryer to 200°C (390°F).
3. Cook the Shrimp: Place the marinated shrimp in the air fryer basket in a single layer. Air fry for 6-8 minutes, or until the shrimp are pink and cooked through.
4. Serve: Sprinkle with fresh parsley and serve with lemon wedges on the side for squeezing over the shrimp.

*Calories: Approximately 250   Protein: 24g.   Fat: 15g. Carbohydrates: 2g.    Fiber: 0g.*

*Ingredients:*
1. 500g large shrimp, peeled and deveined
2. 1/4 cup olive oil
3. 6 cloves garlic, thinly sliced
4. 1 teaspoon red pepper flakes
5. 1 teaspoon smoked paprika
6. Salt to taste
7. 2 tablespoons fresh parsley, chopped
8. 1 lemon, for serving

## French Green Bean Almondine

*Prep: 10min.        Cooking: 15min.        Serves: 4*

*Instructions:*

1. Prepare the Green Beans: Toss the green beans with olive oil, salt, and pepper.
2. Preheat the Air Fryer: Set the air fryer to 180°C (350°F).
3. Cook the Green Beans: Place the green beans in the air fryer basket and cook for 10 minutes, or until tender-crisp.
4. Toast the Almonds: While the beans are cooking, toast the sliced almonds in a dry skillet over medium heat until golden brown, then set aside.
5. Make the Almondine Sauce: In the same skillet, melt the butter and sauté the minced garlic until fragrant. Add the toasted almonds, lemon zest, and lemon juice, and cook for another minute.

*Ingredients:*
1. 500g fresh green beans, trimmed
2. 2 tablespoons olive oil
3. Salt and pepper to taste
4. 1/2 cup sliced almonds
5. 2 tablespoons butter
6. 1 clove garlic, minced
7. 1 lemon, zest and juice
8. Fresh parsley, chopped for garnish

6. Serve: Toss the cooked green beans with the almondine sauce. Garnish with fresh parsley and serve immediately.

*Calories: Approximately 200   Protein: 5g.   Fat: 16g.   Carbohydrates: 12g.     Fiber: 4g.*

# Dinner

## Israeli Herb and Almond Crusted Fish

*Prep: 10min.          Cooking: 12min.          Serves: 4*

*Instructions:*

1. In a bowl, mix the ground almonds, chopped herbs, minced garlic, lemon zest, salt, and pepper.
2. Pat the fish fillets dry with paper towels, then brush each side with olive oil.
3. Press the almond and herb mixture onto one side of each fish fillet to form a crust.
4. Preheat the air fryer to 200°C (390°F).
5. Place the crusted fish fillets in the air fryer basket, herb side up, making sure they are not touching.
6. Cook for about 10-12 minutes, or until the fish is cooked through and the crust is golden brown.
7. Finish with a squeeze of fresh lemon juice before serving.

*Ingredients:*

1. 4 fish fillets (like cod, tilapia, or seabass)
2. 1 cup almonds, finely chopped or ground
3. 1 cup fresh herbs (like parsley, cilantro, and dill), finely chopped
4. 2 garlic cloves, minced
5. 2 tablespoons olive oil
6. 1 lemon, zest and juice
7. Salt and pepper, to taste

*Calories: 350   Protein: 28g.   Fat: 22g.   Carbohydrates: 8g.     Fiber: 4g.*

## Italian Air-Fried Bruschetta Chicken

*Prep: 15min.          Cooking: 15min.          Serves: 4*

*Instructions:*

1. In a bowl, mix the chopped tomatoes, basil, minced garlic, balsamic vinegar, olive oil, salt, and pepper to create the bruschetta topping.
2. Season the chicken breasts with salt and pepper, and brush them lightly with olive oil.
3. Preheat the air fryer to 180°C (350°F).
4. Place the chicken breasts in the air fryer basket and cook for about 10 minutes.
5. After 10 minutes, top each chicken breast with a generous amount of the bruschetta mixture and sprinkle with mozzarella cheese.
6. Return to the air fryer and cook for an additional 5 minutes, or until the cheese is melted and the chicken is fully cooked.
7. The chicken is done when it reaches an internal temperature of 75°C (165°F).

*Ingredients:*

1. 4 boneless, skinless chicken breasts
2. 2 tomatoes, finely chopped
3. 1/4 cup fresh basil leaves, chopped
4. 2 cloves garlic, minced
5. 1/4 cup balsamic vinegar
6. 1/4 cup olive oil
7. Salt and pepper, to taste
8. 1/2 cup shredded mozzarella cheese

*Calories: Approximately 290   Protein: 30g.   Fat: 16g.   Carbohydrates: 6g.     Fiber: 1g.*

# Dinner

## Greek Tzatziki Stuffed Tomatoes

*Prep: 15min.        Cooking: 5min.        Serves: 4*

*Instructions:*

1. Slice off the top of each tomato and carefully hollow out the insides, removing the seeds and pulp to create a cup.
2. In a bowl, combine the Greek yogurt, grated cucumber, minced garlic, chopped dill, olive oil, lemon juice, salt, and pepper to make the tzatziki sauce.
3. Fill each tomato cup with the tzatziki mixture.
4. Preheat the air fryer to 160°C (320°F).
5. Place the stuffed tomatoes in the air fryer basket and cook for about 5 minutes, just until they are warmed through.
6. Serve immediately.

*Ingredients:*

1. 4 large tomatoes
2. 1 cup Greek yogurt
3. 1 cucumber, grated and excess water squeezed out
4. 2 cloves garlic, minced
5. 2 tablespoons fresh dill, chopped
6. 1 tablespoon olive oil
7. 1 tablespoon lemon juice
8. Salt and pepper, to taste

*Calories: 120   Protein: 6g.   Fat: 6g.   Carbohydrates: 12g.     Fiber: 2g.*

## Moroccan Air-Fried Beet Salad with Goat Cheese

*Prep: 10min.        Cooking: 15min.        Serves: 4*

*Instructions:*

1. Toss the sliced beets with olive oil, ground cumin, cinnamon, salt, and pepper.
2. Preheat the air fryer to 180°C (350°F).
3. Arrange the beet slices in the air fryer basket in a single layer. Cook for about 15 minutes, or until tender and slightly crisp at the edges, shaking the basket halfway through.
4. While the beets are cooking, prepare the dressing by whisking together olive oil, lemon juice, honey, salt, and pepper in a small bowl.
5. Once the beets are cooked, let them cool slightly, then transfer to a serving dish.
6. Top the beets with crumbled goat cheese, chopped walnuts, mint, and parsley.
7. Drizzle the prepared dressing over the salad before serving.

*Ingredients:*

1. 4 medium beets, peeled and sliced
2. 1 tablespoon olive oil
3. 1 teaspoon ground cumin
4. 1/2 teaspoon cinnamon
5. Salt and pepper, to taste
6. 1/4 cup walnuts, chopped
7. 1/2 cup goat cheese, crumbled
8. 2 tablespoons fresh mint, chopped
9. 2 tablespoons fresh parsley, chopped
10. For the dressing:
11. 2 tablespoons olive oil
12. 1 tablespoon lemon juice
13. 1 teaspoon honey
14. Salt and pepper, to taste

*Calories: Approximately 250   Protein: 8g.   Fat: 18g.*
*Carbohydrates: 16g.     Fiber: 4g.*

# Dinner

## Portuguese Piri Piri Chicken Wings

*Prep: 15min. (plus marinating time)      Cooking: 25min.      Serves: 4*

*Instructions:*

1. To make the Piri Piri marinade, combine minced garlic, chopped red chilies, paprika, cayenne pepper, lemon juice, red wine vinegar, salt, and pepper in a bowl. Mix well.
2. Toss the chicken wings in the marinade until they are evenly coated. Let them marinate for at least 1 hour, or overnight in the refrigerator for deeper flavor.
3. Preheat the air fryer to 200°C (400°F).
4. Remove the chicken wings from the marinade and shake off excess. Brush the wings with olive oil.
5. Place the wings in the air fryer basket in a single layer. Cook for about 25 minutes, turning halfway through, until the wings are golden brown and crispy.
6. Serve hot, garnished with lemon wedges if desired.

*Ingredients:*
1. 2 lbs chicken wings
2. 2 tablespoons olive oil
3. For the Piri Piri marinade:
4. 4 garlic cloves, minced
5. 2-3 red chilies, finely chopped (adjust to taste)
6. 1 teaspoon paprika
7. 1/2 teaspoon cayenne pepper
8. 1 tablespoon lemon juice
9. 2 tablespoons red wine vinegar
10. Salt and pepper, to taste

*Calories: 450   Protein: 35g.   Fat: 32g.   Carbohydrates: 2g.   Fiber: 0g.*

## Mediterranean Zucchini and Corn Fritters

*Prep: 15min.      Cooking: 10min.      Serves: 4*

*Instructions:*

1. Place the grated zucchini in a colander, sprinkle with a little salt, and let it sit for 10 minutes. Then, squeeze out the excess water.
2. In a large bowl, combine the drained zucchini, corn kernels, flour, grated Parmesan, beaten eggs, minced garlic, parsley, oregano, salt, and pepper. Mix until well combined.
3. Preheat the air fryer to 190°C (375°F) and lightly spray the basket with olive oil.
4. Form the mixture into small patties and place them in the air fryer basket, making sure they don't touch.
5. Cook for about 10 minutes, flipping halfway through, or until the fritters are golden brown and crispy.
6. Serve warm.

*Ingredients:*
1. 2 medium zucchinis, grated
2. 1 cup corn kernels (fresh, canned, or thawed if frozen)
3. 1/2 cup all-purpose flour
4. 1/2 cup grated Parmesan cheese
5. 2 eggs, beaten
6. 2 cloves garlic, minced
7. 1/4 cup fresh parsley, chopped
8. 1 teaspoon dried oregano
9. Salt and pepper, to taste
10. Olive oil spray

*Calories: Approximately 200   Protein: 10g.   Fat: 8g.   Carbohydrates: 24g.   Fiber: 3g.*

# Dinner

## Turkish Pumpkin and Lentil Soup with Air-Fried Croutons

*Prep: 15min.        Cooking: 30min.        Serves: 6*

*Instructions:*

1. In a large pot, heat the olive oil over medium heat. Add the chopped onion and minced garlic, and sauté until soft.
2. Add the pumpkin cubes, lentils, cumin, paprika, salt, and pepper. Stir to combine.
3. Pour in the vegetable broth and bring the mixture to a boil. Then reduce the heat and simmer for about 20 minutes, or until the pumpkin and lentils are tender.
4. While the soup is simmering, prepare the croutons. Toss the bread cubes with olive oil, garlic powder, and salt. Place them in the air fryer basket.
5. Preheat the air fryer to 180°C (350°F). Cook the croutons for about 5 minutes, or until golden and crispy.
6. Use an immersion blender to purée the soup until smooth (or transfer to a blender in batches).
7. Serve the soup hot, topped with air-fried croutons.

*Ingredients:*

1. 1 medium pumpkin (about 2 lbs), peeled and cubed
2. 1 cup red lentils, rinsed
3. 1 large onion, chopped
4. 2 cloves garlic, minced
5. 1 liter vegetable broth
6. 1 teaspoon ground cumin
7. 1 teaspoon paprika
8. Salt and pepper, to taste
9. 2 tablespoons olive oil
10. For the croutons:
11. 2 slices of bread, cubed
12. 1 tablespoon olive oil
13. 1/2 teaspoon garlic powder
14. Salt to taste

*Calories: 280    Protein: 12g.   Fat: 8g.   Carbohydrates: 44g.     Fiber: 12g.*

## Spanish Egg and Potato Tortilla

*Prep: 15min.        Cooking: 25min.        Serves: 4*

*Instructions:*

1. Preheat the air fryer to 180°C (350°F).
2. In a bowl, toss the thinly sliced potatoes and onion with olive oil, salt, and pepper.
3. Place the potato and onion mixture in the air fryer basket and cook for about 15 minutes, or until the potatoes are tender, stirring halfway through.
4. In a large bowl, beat the eggs and season with salt and pepper. Add the cooked potato and onion mixture to the eggs and stir to combine.

*Ingredients:*

1. 4 large eggs
2. 2 medium potatoes, thinly sliced
3. 1 onion, thinly sliced
4. 1/4 cup olive oil
5. Salt and pepper, to taste

5. Place a piece of parchment paper in the air fryer basket and pour in the egg and potato mixture, spreading it evenly.
6. Cook for about 10 minutes, or until the eggs are set and the tortilla is lightly golden on top.
7. Carefully remove the tortilla from the air fryer and let it cool slightly before cutting into wedges.

*Calories: Approximately 300    Protein: 10g.   Fat: 20g.   Carbohydrates: 20g.     Fiber: 2g.*

# Dinner

## Italian Sausage and Pepper Sliders

*Prep: 10min.     Cooking: 15min.     Serves: 6*

*Instructions:*

1. Preheat the air fryer to 200°C (400°F).
2. In a bowl, toss the sausage pieces, sliced bell peppers, and onion with olive oil, salt, and pepper.
3. Place the sausage and vegetable mixture in the air fryer basket. Cook for about 15 minutes, or until the sausage is cooked through and the vegetables are tender and slightly charred, shaking the basket halfway through cooking.
4. If you want to add cheese, place a slice on each sausage piece during the last 2 minutes of cooking to melt.
5. Assemble the sliders by placing a piece of sausage and some of the pepper and onion mixture on each mini bun. Add marinara sauce if desired.
6. Serve hot.

*Ingredients:*

1. 1 pound Italian sausage, cut into 1-inch pieces
2. 1 red bell pepper, sliced
3. 1 green bell pepper, sliced
4. 1 onion, sliced
5. 2 tablespoons olive oil
6. Salt and pepper, to taste
7. Mini slider buns
8. Optional: cheese slices, marinara sauce

*Calories: 350   Protein: 16g.   Fat: 25g.   Carbohydrates: 15g.     Fiber: 1g.*


## Greek Air-Fried Feta Cheese with Honey and Sesame

*Prep: 5min.     Cooking: 10min.     Serves: 4*

*Instructions:*

1. Preheat the air fryer to 180°C (350°F).
2. Brush the block of feta cheese with olive oil and coat it evenly with sesame seeds on all sides.
3. Place the coated feta in the air fryer basket and cook for about 10 minutes, or until the cheese is heated through and the sesame seeds are golden brown.
4. Carefully remove the feta from the air fryer, drizzle with honey, and garnish with fresh thyme or oregano if desired.
5. Serve warm as an appetizer or part of a cheese board.

*Ingredients:*

1. 1 block of feta cheese (about 200 grams or 7 ounces)
2. 2 tablespoons olive oil
3. 3 tablespoons sesame seeds
4. 2 tablespoons honey
5. Fresh thyme or oregano for garnish (optional)

*Calories: Approximately 250   Protein: 10g.   Fat: 20g.   Carbohydrates: 10g.     Fiber: 1g.*

# Dinner

## Egyptian Air-Fried Kofta

*Prep: 15min.     Cooking: 10min.     Serves: 4*

*Instructions:*

1. In a bowl, combine the ground meat, onion, garlic, parsley, cumin, paprika, cinnamon, salt, and pepper. Mix well.
2. Form the mixture into elongated patties or sausage shapes.
3. Preheat the air fryer to 200°C (390°F).
4. Place the kofta in the air fryer basket, ensuring they are not touching.
5. Cook for about 10 minutes, turning halfway through, or until cooked through and browned on the outside.

*Ingredients:*

1. 500g (1 lb) ground lamb or beef
2. 1 onion, finely chopped
3. 2 cloves garlic, minced
4. 2 tablespoons fresh parsley, chopped
5. 1 teaspoon ground cumin
6. 1 teaspoon paprika
7. 1/2 teaspoon ground cinnamon
8. Salt and pepper, to taste

*Calories: 300   Protein: 24g.   Fat: 20g.   Carbohydrates: 5g.     Fiber: 1g.*

## French Dijon and Thyme Roasted Chicken

*Prep: 10min.     Cooking: 25min.     Serves: 4*

*Instructions:*

1. In a bowl, mix the Dijon mustard, olive oil, thyme, salt, and pepper to create a marinade.
2. Coat the chicken thighs evenly with the marinade and let them rest for at least 15 minutes.
3. Preheat the air fryer to 190°C (375°F).
4. Place the chicken thighs skin-side up in the air fryer basket, and scatter lemon slices around the chicken.
5. Cook for about 25 minutes, or until the chicken is golden brown and the internal temperature reaches 75°C (165°F).

*Ingredients:*

1. 4 chicken thighs, skin on
2. 2 tablespoons Dijon mustard
3. 1 tablespoon olive oil
4. 1 teaspoon dried thyme
5. Salt and pepper, to taste
6. 1 lemon, sliced

*Calories: Approximately 400   Protein: 28g.   Fat: 30g.   Carbohydrates: 2g.     Fiber: 0g.*

# Dinner

## Croatian Air-Fried Fish with Garlic and Parsley

*Prep: 10min.      Cooking: 12min.      Serves: 4*

*Instructions:*

1. Pat the fish fillets dry with paper towels. Season with salt and pepper.
2. In a small bowl, mix the minced garlic, chopped parsley, and olive oil.
3. Brush the garlic and parsley mixture onto both sides of the fish fillets.
4. Preheat the air fryer to 180°C (350°F).
5. Place the fish fillets in the air fryer basket in a single layer.
6. Cook for about 12 minutes, flipping halfway through, or until the fish is cooked through and flakes easily with a fork.
7. Serve immediately with lemon wedges on the side.

*Ingredients:*

1. 4 fish fillets (such as sea bass, cod, or hake)
2. 4 cloves garlic, minced
3. 1/4 cup fresh parsley, chopped
4. 2 tablespoons olive oil
5. Salt and pepper, to taste
6. Lemon wedges, for serving

*Calories: 200   Protein: 22g.   Fat: 10g.   Carbohydrates: 2g.    Fiber: 0g.*


## Algerian Air-Fried Carrot Fritters

*Prep: 15min.      Cooking: 10min.      Serves: 4*

*Instructions:*

1. In a large bowl, combine the grated carrots, flour, eggs, cumin, paprika, salt, and pepper. Mix well to form a thick batter.
2. Preheat the air fryer to 190°C (375°F) and lightly spray the basket with olive oil.
3. Form small patties from the mixture and place them in the air fryer basket, ensuring they are not touching.
4. Cook for about 10 minutes, flipping halfway through, until golden brown and crispy.
5. Serve hot.

*Ingredients:*

1. 2 cups grated carrots
2. 1/2 cup all-purpose flour
3. 2 eggs
4. 1/2 teaspoon ground cumin
5. 1/2 teaspoon paprika
6. Salt and pepper, to taste
7. Olive oil spray

*Calories: Approximately 150   Protein: 5g.   Fat: 5g.   Carbohydrates: 20g.    Fiber: 3g.*

# Dinner

## Italian Air-Fried Polenta Cake with Marinara

*Prep: 5min.      Cooking: 15min.      Serves: 4*

*Instructions:*

1. Preheat the air fryer to 200°C (390°F).
2. Brush both sides of the polenta slices with olive oil and season with salt and pepper.
3. Place the polenta slices in the air fryer basket in a single layer.
4. Cook for about 15 minutes, flipping halfway through, until the polenta is golden and crispy.
5. Warm the marinara sauce in a saucepan or microwave.
6. Serve the crispy polenta topped with warm marinara sauce and sprinkled with grated Parmesan cheese. Garnish with fresh basil.

*Ingredients:*

1. 1 tube of pre-cooked polenta, sliced into rounds
2. 1 cup marinara sauce
3. 1/2 cup grated Parmesan cheese
4. 2 tablespoons olive oil
5. Salt and pepper, to taste
6. Fresh basil for garnish

*Calories: 250   Protein: 6g.   Fat: 12g.   Carbohydrates: 30g.      Fiber: 2g.*

## Greek Air-Fried Lamb Meatballs with Tzatziki

*Prep: 15min.      Cooking: 15min.      Serves: 4*

*Instructions:*

15. In a bowl, combine the ground lamb, grated onion, minced garlic, chopped mint, oregano, salt, and pepper. Mix well.
16. Form the mixture into small meatballs.
17. Preheat the air fryer to 190°C (375°F) and lightly spray the basket with olive oil.
18. Place the meatballs in the air fryer basket, ensuring they are not touching.
19. Cook for about 15 minutes, turning halfway through, until the meatballs are browned and cooked through.
20. For the tzatziki, combine Greek yogurt, grated cucumber, minced garlic, chopped dill, lemon juice, and salt in a bowl. Mix well.
21. Serve the meatballs with the tzatziki sauce on the side.

*Ingredients:*

1. 500g (1 lb) ground lamb
2. 1 onion, finely grated
3. 2 cloves garlic, minced
4. 2 tablespoons fresh mint, chopped
5. 1 teaspoon dried oregano
6. Salt and pepper, to taste
7. Olive oil spray
8. For the tzatziki:
9. 1 cup Greek yogurt
10. 1/2 cucumber, grated and drained
11. 1 clove garlic, minced
12. 2 tablespoons fresh dill, chopped
13. 1 tablespoon lemon juice
14. Salt to taste

*Calories: Approximately 400   Protein: 24g.   Fat: 30g.*
*Carbohydrates: 10g.      Fiber: 1g.*

# Dinner

## Spanish Manchego and Quince Paste Bites

*Prep: 5min.     Cooking: 2min.     Serves: 4*

*Instructions:*

1. Slice the Manchego cheese and quince paste into small, bite-sized pieces.
2. Preheat the air fryer to 180°C (350°F).
3. Place a slice of quince paste on top of each slice of Manchego cheese.
4. Carefully place the bites in the air fryer basket and cook for just 2 minutes, or until the cheese begins to melt slightly.
5. Serve immediately on crackers or bread slices.

*Ingredients:*
1. 200g Manchego cheese, sliced
2. 200g quince paste, sliced
3. Crackers or bread slices for serving

*Calories: 300   Protein: 15g.   Fat: 20g.   Carbohydrates: 20g.     Fiber: 0g.*

## Lebanese Air-Fried Spinach Pies (Fatayer)

*Prep: 20min.     Cooking: 10min.     Serves: 4*

*Instructions:*

13. To make the dough, mix flour, salt, olive oil, and water in a bowl to form a smooth dough. Let it rest for 15 minutes.
14. For the filling, combine the spinach, onion, pine nuts, sumac, salt, pepper, lemon juice, and olive oil in a bowl.
15. Preheat the air fryer to 190°C (375°F).
16. Divide the dough into small balls, roll each into a circle, and place some filling in the center of each.
17. Fold the edges over to form a triangle or square, sealing the filling inside.
18. Place the pies in the air fryer basket, ensuring they are not touching, and cook for about 10 minutes, or until golden and crispy.
19. Serve hot.

*Ingredients:*
*For the dough:*
1. 2 cups all-purpose flour
2. 1/2 teaspoon salt
3. 1 tablespoon olive oil
4. 3/4 cup water
5. For the filling:
6. 2 cups spinach, chopped
7. 1 onion, finely chopped
8. 2 tablespoons pine nuts (optional)
9. 1 teaspoon sumac
10. Salt and pepper, to taste
11. 2 tablespoons lemon juice
12. 2 tablespoons olive oil

*Calories: Approximately 350   Protein: 8g.   Fat: 15g. Carbohydrates: 45g.     Fiber: 3g.*

# Dinner

## Turkish Air-Fried Zucchini Pancakes (Mücver)

*Prep: 15min.     Cooking: 10min.     Serves: 4*

*Instructions:*

1. Squeeze the excess water out of the grated zucchinis.
2. In a large bowl, combine the drained zucchinis, grated onion, eggs, flour, crumbled feta cheese, chopped dill, parsley, salt, and pepper. Mix well to form a batter.
3. Preheat the air fryer to 190°C (375°F).
4. Shape the batter into small pancakes and place them in the air fryer basket, sprayed with a little olive oil to prevent sticking.
5. Cook for about 10 minutes, flipping halfway through, until the pancakes are golden brown and crispy on the outside.
6. Serve hot.

*Calories: 200   Protein: 9g.   Fat: 9g.   Carbohydrates: 20g. Fiber: 2g.*

*Ingredients:*

1. 2 medium zucchinis, grated and drained
2. 1 small onion, grated
3. 2 eggs
4. 1/2 cup all-purpose flour
5. 1/2 cup feta cheese, crumbled
6. 2 tablespoons fresh dill, chopped
7. 2 tablespoons fresh parsley, chopped
8. Salt and pepper, to taste
9. Olive oil spray

## French Provencal Vegetable Tart

*Prep: 20min.     Cooking: 20min.     Serves: 4*

*Instructions:*

10. Preheat the air fryer to 180°C (350°F).
11. Roll out the puff pastry to fit the air fryer basket and place it inside.
12. Arrange the sliced vegetables (zucchini, eggplant, tomato, bell pepper) on the puff pastry.
13. Drizzle with olive oil and sprinkle with herbs de Provence, salt, and pepper.
14. Cook in the air fryer for about 20 minutes, or until the pastry is golden brown and the vegetables are tender.
15. Sprinkle grated Parmesan over the tart in the last few minutes of cooking.
16. Serve hot or at room temperature.

*Ingredients:*

1. 1 sheet of puff pastry
2. 1 small zucchini, thinly sliced
3. 1 small eggplant, thinly sliced
4. 1 tomato, thinly sliced
5. 1 bell pepper, thinly sliced
6. 2 tablespoons olive oil
7. 2 teaspoons herbs de Provence
8. Salt and pepper, to taste
9. 1/4 cup grated Parmesan cheese

*Calories: Approximately 350   Protein: 8g.   Fat: 2g.   Carbohydrates: 30g.   Fiber: 3g.*

# Dinner

## Moroccan Air-Fried Stuffed Dates with Almond and Cream Cheese

*Prep: 15min.      Cooking: 5min.      Serves: 20 dates*

*Instructions:*

1. Open the pitted dates slightly and stuff each one with a small amount of cream cheese.
2. Insert an almond into the center of the cream cheese in each date.
3. Preheat the air fryer to 160°C (320°F).
4. Place the stuffed dates in the air fryer basket and cook for about 5 minutes, or until the dates are warm and slightly softened.
5. Garnish with crushed pistachios and a drizzle of honey if desired.
6. Serve warm or at room temperature.

*Ingredients:*

1. 20 Medjool dates, pitted
2. 1/2 cup cream cheese, softened
3. 20 almonds, toasted
4. 1/4 cup crushed pistachios for garnish (optional)
5. Honey for drizzling (optional)

*Calories: 100   Protein: 2g.   Fat: 3g.   Carbohydrates: 18g.   Fiber: 2g.*

## Italian Air-Fried Veal Milanese

*Prep: 15min.      Cooking: 10min.      Serves: 4*

*Instructions:*

7. Season the veal cutlets with salt and pepper.
8. Dredge each cutlet in flour, dip in beaten eggs, and then coat with breadcrumbs.
9. Preheat the air fryer to 200°C (390°F).
10. Place the breaded cutlets in the air fryer basket, making sure they are not overlapping.
11. Cook for about 10 minutes, flipping halfway through, until the cutlets are golden brown and cooked through.
12. Serve hot with lemon wedges on the side.

*Ingredients:*

1. 4 veal cutlets, pounded thin
2. 1 cup all-purpose flour
3. 2 eggs, beaten
4. 2 cups breadcrumbs
5. Salt and pepper, to taste
6. Lemon wedges, for serving

*Calories: Approximately 450   Protein: 30g.   Fat: 15g.   Carbohydrates: 45g.   Fiber: 2g.*

# Dinner

## Greek Air-Fried Octopus with Vinegar and Oregano

*Prep: 10min.      Cooking: 15min.      Serves: 4*

*Instructions:*
1. Preheat the air fryer to 200°C (390°F).
2. Toss the octopus tentacles with olive oil, red wine vinegar, oregano, salt, and pepper.
3. Place the tentacles in the air fryer basket in a single layer.
4. Cook for about 15 minutes, turning once midway, until the octopus is tender and slightly crispy on the edges.
5. Serve hot, garnished with lemon wedges.

*Ingredients:*
1. 1 lb octopus, cleaned and tentacles separated
2. 2 tablespoons olive oil
3. 2 tablespoons red wine vinegar
4. 1 teaspoon dried oregano
5. Salt and pepper, to taste
6. Lemon wedges for serving

*Calories: 150    Protein: 25g.    Fat: 5g.    Carbohydrates: 2g. Fiber: 0g.*

## Mediterranean Air-Fried Shrimp with Herbs and Garlic

*Prep: 10min.      Cooking: 8min.      Serves: 4*

*Instructions:*
9. In a bowl, combine shrimp, olive oil, minced garlic, basil, oregano, red pepper flakes, salt, and pepper, tossing to coat evenly.
10. Preheat the air fryer to 180°C (350°F).
11. Place the shrimp in the air fryer basket in a single layer.
12. Cook for about 8 minutes, shaking the basket halfway through, until the shrimp are pink and cooked through.
13. Serve hot, garnished with lemon wedges.

*Ingredients:*
1. 1 lb large shrimp, peeled and deveined
2. 3 tablespoons olive oil
3. 4 cloves garlic, minced
4. 1 teaspoon dried basil
5. 1 teaspoon dried oregano
6. 1/2 teaspoon red pepper flakes
7. Salt and pepper, to taste
8. Lemon wedges for serving

*Calories: Approximately 200    Protein: 24g.    Fat: 10g. Carbohydrates: 2g.    Fiber: 0g.*

# 30 Bonus Salads

Mediterranean cuisine is a treasure trove of flavors, emphasizing fresh ingredients and simple preparations that highlight natural tastes and nutritional benefits. Here's a deeper look into the essence of these Mediterranean dishes:

Greek Salad is a classic, embodying the Mediterranean ethos with its use of ripe tomatoes, crisp cucumbers, sharp red onions, briny olives, and creamy feta cheese, all brought together with a drizzle of olive oil and a sprinkle of oregano.

Tabbouleh is a herbaceous delight, primarily featuring parsley, with mint, tomatoes, and bulgur wheat, offering a light yet satisfying dish that's perfect for hot weather, demonstrating the region's penchant for fresh, aromatic herbs.

Fattoush represents the resourceful nature of Mediterranean cooking, turning leftover pita bread into a crunchy component of a salad bursting with the flavors of mixed vegetables and a sumac-infused dressing.

Mediterranean Chickpea Salad is a testament to the region's love for legumes, combining hearty chickpeas with a colorful array of vegetables and a lemony dressing, showcasing the diet's balance between protein, fiber, and vitamins.

Panzanella, an Italian staple, transforms stale bread and seasonal vegetables into a vibrant salad, soaked in a tangy vinaigrette, illustrating the Mediterranean knack for waste reduction and flavor maximization.

These recipes not only offer a culinary journey through the Mediterranean landscape but also reflect the dietary principles that make this region's cuisine one of the most healthful and enjoyable in the world. The emphasis on vegetables, whole grains, and healthy fats, along with moderate protein from legumes and dairy, encapsulates a diet that's as nourishing as it is delightful. Through these dishes, one can taste the sun-drenched shores, the aromatic markets, and the timeless traditions that define Mediterranean cooking.

# Salads

## Greek Salad

*Prep: 15min.       Cooking: 0min.       Serves: 4*

*Instructions:*

1. In a large salad bowl, combine tomatoes, cucumbers, red onion, and olives. Top with feta cheese, drizzle with olive oil, vinegar if using, and sprinkle with oregano. Season with salt and pepper. Gently toss to combine.

*Calories: 200   Protein: 6g.   Fat: 16g.   Carbohydrates: 10g. Fiber: 2g.*

*Ingredients:*

1. 4 medium ripe tomatoes, cut into wedges
2. 1 cucumber, sliced
3. 1 red onion, thinly sliced
4. 1/2 cup kalamata olives
5. 200g feta cheese, cut into cubes or crumbled
6. 3 tablespoons extra virgin olive oil
7. 1 tablespoon red wine vinegar (optional)
8. 1 teaspoon dried oregano
9. Salt and pepper to taste

## Fattoush

*Prep: 20min.       Cooking: 0min.       Serves: 4*

*Instructions:*

1. In a large mixing bowl, combine lettuce, tomatoes, cucumbers, and radishes.
2. In a separate small bowl, whisk together olive oil, lemon juice, sumac, salt, and pepper to create the dressing.
3. Pour the dressing over the salad and toss to coat.
4. Just before serving, add the crispy pita bread and toss again.

*Calories: Approximately 150   Protein: 3g.   Fat: 7g. Carbohydrates: 18g.     Fiber: 3g.*

*Ingredients:*

1. 1 head romaine lettuce, chopped
2. 2 medium tomatoes, diced
3. 2 cucumbers, diced
4. 4 radishes, thinly sliced
5. 2 pieces of pita bread, toasted or fried until crispy and broken into pieces
6. 1 teaspoon ground sumac
7. 2 tablespoons olive oil
8. 1 tablespoon lemon juice
9. Salt and pepper to taste

# Salads

## Chickpea Salad

*Prep: 15min.        Cooking: 0min.        Serves: 4*

*Instructions:*
1. In a large bowl, combine chickpeas, cucumber, bell pepper, and red onion.
2. Drizzle with olive oil and lemon juice, then sprinkle with salt and pepper.
3. Toss the salad to ensure even coating of the dressing.
4. Gently fold in the feta cheese just before serving.

*Calories: 250   Protein: 9g.   Fat: 14g.   Carbohydrates: 23g. Fiber: 6g.*

*Ingredients:*
1. 1 can chickpeas (15 ounces), drained and rinsed
2. 1 cucumber, diced
3. 1 bell pepper, diced
4. 1 small red onion, finely chopped
5. 1/2 cup feta cheese, crumbled
6. 3 tablespoons olive oil
7. 2 tablespoons lemon juice
8. Salt and pepper to taste

## Italian Panzanella

*Prep: 20min.        Cooking: 0min.        Serves: 4*

*Instructions:*
1. If the bread isn't stale, toast the bread cubes in the oven until lightly crisp.
2. In a large bowl, combine the tomatoes, onions, and cucumbers.
3. In a small bowl, whisk together olive oil, vinegar, mustard, salt, and pepper to make the vinaigrette.
4. Pour the vinaigrette over the vegetables, and let them marinate for about 10 minutes.
5. Add the bread cubes and torn basil to the bowl, toss everything to coat with the vinaigrette and let the mixture sit for another 10 minutes for the flavors to meld and the bread to absorb the dressing.

*Calories: Approximately 350   Protein: 8g.   Fat: 18g. Carbohydrates: 140g.    Fiber: 3g.*

*Ingredients:*
1. 4 cups stale bread, preferably sourdough or ciabatta, cut into 1-inch cubes
2. 4 medium ripe tomatoes, cut into chunks
3. 1 small red onion, thinly sliced
4. 1 cucumber, seeded and sliced
5. 1 bunch of fresh basil leaves, torn into small pieces

For the vinaigrette:
6. 1/4 cup extra virgin olive oil
7. 2 tablespoons balsamic vinegar or red wine vinegar
8. 1 teaspoon Dijon mustard
9. Salt and pepper to taste

# Salads

## Israeli Couscous Salad

*Prep: 10min.     Cooking: 10min.     Serves: 4*

*Instructions:*
1. Cook the couscous in water or vegetable broth according to package instructions until al dente, then it down.
2. In a large bowl, combine the cooked couscous, cherry tomatoes, cucumber, and parsley.
3. In a small bowl, whisk together olive oil, lemon juice, and pepper to make the vinaigrette.
4. Pour the vinaigrette over the salad and toss to combine.

*Ingredients:*
1. 1 cup pearl couscous
2. 2 cups water or vegetable broth                                    cool
3. 1 cup cherry tomatoes, halved
4. 1 cucumber, diced
5. 1/2 cup parsley, chopped                    salt,
6. For the lemon vinaigrette:
7. 3 tablespoons olive oil
8. 1 lemon, juiced
9. Salt and pepper to taste

*Calories: Approximately 250   Protein: 7g.  Fat: 7g.  Carbohydrates: 41g.    Fiber: 3g.*

## Moroccan Carrot Salad

*Prep: 15min.     Cooking: 0min.     Serves: 4*

*Instructions:*
1. In a large bowl, combine the grated carrots, raisins, toasted almonds.
2. In a small bowl, whisk together the olive oil, orange juice, lemon juice, cinnamon, honey (if using), and to make the dressing.
3. Pour the dressing over the carrot mixture and toss to combine.
4. Chill in the refrigerator before serving to allow flavors meld.

*Ingredients:*
1. 4 cups grated carrots                                    and
2. 1/2 cup raisins
3. 1/4 cup slivered almonds, toasted
4. 1/2 teaspoon ground cinnamon                            salt
5. For the orange dressing:
6. 3 tablespoons olive oil                                  well
7. 2 tablespoons orange juice, freshly squeezed            to
8. 1 tablespoon lemon juice
9. 1 teaspoon honey (optional)

*Calories: Approximately 200   Protein: 3g.  Fat: 9g. Carbohydrates: 31g.    Fiber: 5g.*

# Salads

## Fattoush

*Prep: 20min.      Cooking: 0min.      Serves: 4*

*Instructions:*

5. In a large mixing bowl, combine lettuce, tomatoes, cucumbers, and radishes.
6. In a separate small bowl, whisk together olive oil, lemon juice, sumac, salt, and pepper to create the dressing.
7. Pour the dressing over the salad and toss to coat.
8. Just before serving, add the crispy pita bread and toss again.

*Calories: Approximately 150   Protein: 3g.  Fat: 7g. Carbohydrates: 18g.     Fiber: 3g.*

*Ingredients:*
10. 1 head romaine lettuce, chopped
11. 2 medium tomatoes, diced
12. 2 cucumbers, diced
13. 4 radishes, thinly sliced
14. 2 pieces of pita bread, toasted or fried until crispy and broken into pieces
15. 1 teaspoon ground sumac
16. 2 tablespoons olive oil
17. 1 tablespoon lemon juice
18. Salt and pepper to taste

## Turkish White Bean Salad

*Prep: 15min.      Cooking: 0min.      Serves: 4*

*Instructions:*

1. In a large bowl, mix the white beans, tomatoes, onions, and parsley.
2. In a small bowl, whisk together olive oil, vinegar, sumac, and salt to create the dressing.
3. Pour the dressing over the bean mixture and toss to coat.
4. Let the salad sit for a few minutes before serving to allow the flavors to come together.

*Calories: Approximately 220   Protein: 10g.  Fat: 7g. Carbohydrates: 33g.     Fiber: 9g.*

*Ingredients:*
1. 2 cups cooked white beans (or one 15-ounce can, drained and rinsed)
2. 2 medium tomatoes, diced
3. 1 small onion, finely chopped
4. 1/2 cup parsley, chopped
5. For the sumac dressing:
6. 3 tablespoons olive oil
7. 1 tablespoon vinegar
8. 1 teaspoon ground sumac
9. Salt to taste

# Salads

## Cypriot Grain Salad

*Prep: 15min.       Cooking: 20min.       Serves: 4*

*Instructions:*

1. Cook the freekeh or bulgur in water or broth according to package instructions until tender, then let it cool.
2. In a large bowl, combine the cooled grains, pomegranate seeds, toasted almonds, and chopped herbs.
3. In a small bowl, whisk together the olive oil, lemon juice, orange juice, zest, salt, and pepper to make the dressing.
4. Pour the dressing over the salad and toss to combine thoroughly.

*Calories: Approximately 330    Protein: 9g.   Fat: 14g.*
*Carbohydrates: 45g.    Fiber: 9g.*

*Ingredients:*
1. 1 cup freekeh or bulgur, rinsed
2. 2 cups water or vegetable broth
3. 1/2 cup pomegranate seeds
4. 1/2 cup almonds, chopped and toasted
5. 1/2 cup fresh herbs (such as parsley, mint, and cilantro), chopped
6. For the citrus dressing:
7. 3 tablespoons olive oil
8. 2 tablespoons lemon juice
9. 1 orange, zested and juiced
10. Salt and pepper to taste

## Spanish Gazpacho Salad

*Prep: 15min.       Cooking: 0min.       Serves: 4*

*Instructions:*

1. In a large bowl, combine the chopped tomatoes, cucumber, bell pepper, and red onion.
2. In a small bowl, whisk together the olive oil, sherry vinegar, minced garlic, salt, and pepper to create the dressing.
3. Pour the dressing over the vegetables and toss gently to coat.
4. Let the salad sit for a few minutes to allow the flavors to blend before serving.

*Calories: Approximately 180    Protein: 5g.   Fat: 7g.*
*Carbohydrates: 33g.    Fiber: 4g.*

*Ingredients:*
1. 4 large tomatoes, chopped
2. 1 cucumber, seeded and chopped
3. 1 green bell pepper, chopped
4. 1 small red onion, chopped
5. For the sherry vinegar dressing:
6. 1/4 cup olive oil
7. 2 tablespoons sherry vinegar
8. 1 clove garlic, minced
9. Salt and pepper to taste

# Salads

## Potato Salad

*Prep: 20min.     Cooking: 15min.     Serves: 4*

*Instructions:*

1. Boil the potatoes in salted water until just tender, about 10-15 minutes. In the last 4 minutes of cooking, add the green beans to the pot.
2. Drain and let cool slightly.
3. In a small bowl, whisk together the olive oil, vinegar, mustard, garlic, salt, and pepper to make the dressing.
4. In a large bowl, combine the potatoes, green beans, olives, and capers.
5. Pour the dressing over the salad and gently toss to combine.
6. Garnish with fresh parsley before serving.

*Calories: Approximately 300   Protein: 4g.   Fat: 14g.
Carbohydrates: 40g.     Fiber: 6g.*

*Ingredients:*

1. 1.5 pounds of potatoes, peeled and cut into bite-sized pieces
2. 1/2 cup pitted kalamata olives, halved
3. 1 cup green beans, trimmed and halved
4. 2 tablespoons capers, rinsed
5. 1/4 cup extra virgin olive oil
6. 2 tablespoons white wine vinegar
7. 1 teaspoon Dijon mustard
8. 1 garlic clove, minced
9. Salt and pepper to taste
10. Fresh parsley, chopped (for garnish)

## Lebanese Moussaka Salad

*Prep: 15min.     Cooking: 20min.     Serves: 4*

*Instructions:*

12. Preheat your oven to 400°F (200°C). Toss the cubed eggplant with olive oil and salt, and spread it out on a baking sheet.
13. Roast the eggplant for about 20 minutes or until tender and starting to brown.
14. Let the eggplant cool slightly, then combine with the chickpeas and tomatoes in a large bowl.
15. In a small bowl, whisk together the tahini paste, lemon juice, minced garlic, water, salt, and pepper to create the dressing. Adjust the water to achieve the desired consistency.
16. Drizzle the dressing over the salad and toss gently to coat everything evenly.

*Calories: Approximately 350   Protein: 9g.   Fat: 15g.
Carbohydrates: 50g.     Fiber: 14g.*

*Ingredients:*

1. 2 large eggplants, cubed
2. 1 can (15 ounces) chickpeas, drained and rinsed
3. 2 large tomatoes, diced
4. 1 tablespoon olive oil
5. Salt to taste
6. For the tahini dressing:
7. 1/4 cup tahini paste
8. 2 tablespoons lemon juice
9. 1 garlic clove, minced
10. 3-4 tablespoons water (as needed for consistency)
11. Salt and pepper to taste

# Salads

## Pasta Salad

*Prep: 15min.      Cooking: 10min.      Serves: 4*

*Instructions:*
1. Cook the pasta according to package instructions until al dente. Rinse under cold water to cool and stop the cooking process.
2. In a large bowl, combine the cooled pasta, sun-dried tomatoes, olives, and crumbled feta.
3. In a separate small bowl, mix the pesto, olive oil, and lemon juice to create the dressing. Season with salt and pepper.
4. Pour the dressing over the pasta mixture and toss to coat evenly.
5. Garnish with toasted pine nuts for added texture and flavor if desired.
6. Chill in the refrigerator for at least 30 minutes before serving to allow the flavors to meld together.

*Calories: Approximately 450   Protein:1 4g.   Fat: 20g. Carbohydrates: 55g.    Fiber: 3g.*

*Ingredients:*
1. 8 ounces pasta (such as penne, fusilli, or farfalle)
2. 1/2 cup sun-dried tomatoes, chopped
3. 1/2 cup Kalamata olives, pitted and sliced
4. 1/2 cup feta cheese, crumbled
5. 1/4 cup pine nuts, toasted (optional)
6. For the pesto dressing:
7. 1/2 cup basil pesto (store-bought or homemade)
8. 2 tablespoons extra virgin olive oil
9. 1 tablespoon lemon juice
10. Salt and pepper to taste

## Caprese Salad

*Prep: 10min.      Cooking: 0min.      Serves: 4*

*Instructions:*
6. Arrange the tomato and mozzarella slices alternately on a serving platter or individual plates.
7. Place fresh basil leaves on top of the tomato and mozzarella slices.
8. Drizzle balsamic glaze over the salad.
9. Season with salt and pepper if desired.
10. Serve immediately.

*Ingredients:*
1. 2 large tomatoes, sliced
2. 1 pound fresh mozzarella cheese, sliced
3. 1 bunch fresh basil leaves
4. Balsamic glaze (store-bought or homemade)
5. Salt and pepper to taste (optional)

*Calories: Approximately 280   Protein: 20g.   Fat: 20g.   Carbohydrates: 10g.    Fiber: 2g.*

# Salads

## Greek Orzo Salad

*Prep: 15min.     Cooking: 10min.     Serves: 4*

*Instructions:*

1. Cook the orzo pasta according to package instructions until al dente. Drain and rinse under cold water.
2. In a large mixing bowl, combine the cooked orzo, diced cucumber, halved cherry tomatoes, sliced Kalamata olives, and crumbled feta cheese.
3. Prepare the lemon-oregano dressing by whisking together lemon juice, olive oil, dried oregano, salt, and pepper in a small bowl.
4. Pour the dressing over the salad ingredients and toss until well combined.
5. Season with salt and pepper to taste, if desired.
6. Chill in the refrigerator for at least 30 minutes before serving to allow the flavors to meld.
7. Serve chilled as a side dish or light meal.

*Ingredients:*
1. 1 cup orzo pasta
2. 1 cucumber, diced
3. 1 cup cherry tomatoes, halved
4. 1/2 cup Kalamata olives, sliced
5. 1/2 cup crumbled feta cheese
6. Lemon-oregano dressing (made with lemon juice, olive oil, dried oregano, salt, and pepper)
7. Salt and pepper to taste (optional)

*Calories: Approximately 320   Protein: 9g.   Fat: 12g.   Carbohydrates: 45g.   Fiber: 4g.*

## Eggplant and Pomegranate Salad

*Prep: 15min.     Cooking: 25min.     Serves: 4*

*Instructions:*

7. Preheat the oven to 400°F (200°C).
8. Spread the diced eggplant on a baking sheet lined with parchment paper. Drizzle with olive oil and season with salt and pepper.
9. Roast the eggplant in the preheated oven for 20-25 minutes, or until tender and golden brown.
10. While the eggplant is roasting, prepare the yogurt dressing by mixing Greek yogurt, lemon juice, minced garlic, salt, and pepper in a small bowl. Adjust seasoning to taste.

*Ingredients:*
1. 1 large eggplant, diced
2. 1 cup pomegranate seeds
3. 1/2 cup walnuts, chopped
4. Yogurt dressing (made with Greek yogurt, lemon juice, garlic, salt, and pepper)
5. Olive oil for roasting
6. Salt and pepper to taste (optional)

11. Once the eggplant is roasted, remove it from the oven and let it cool slightly.
12. In a large mixing bowl, combine the roasted eggplant, pomegranate seeds, and chopped walnuts.
13. Drizzle the yogurt dressing over the salad ingredients and toss until well coated.
14. Serve immediately as a side dish or light meal.

*Calories: Approximately 280   Protein: 8g.   Fat: 15g.   Carbohydrates: 30g.   Fiber: 8g.*

# Salads

## Quinoa Salad

*Prep: 15min.     Cooking: 15min.     Serves: 4*

*Instructions:*

1. Rinse the quinoa under cold water using a fine-mesh strainer.
2. In a medium saucepan, bring 2 cups of water to a boil. Add the rinsed quinoa and reduce the heat to low. Cover and simmer for 12-15 minutes, or until the quinoa is cooked and the water is absorbed.
3. Remove the cooked quinoa from the heat and let it cool to room temperature.
4. In a large mixing bowl, combine the cooked quinoa, chopped artichoke hearts, and chopped sun-dried tomatoes.
5. Prepare the lemon dressing by whisking together lemon juice, olive oil, minced garlic, salt, and pepper in a small bowl.
6. Pour the dressing over the salad ingredients and toss until well combined.
7. Season with salt and pepper to taste, if desired.
8. Chill in the refrigerator for at least 30 minutes before serving to allow the flavors to meld.
9. Serve chilled as a side dish or light meal.

*Ingredients:*
1. 1 cup quinoa
2. 1 can (14 oz) artichoke hearts, drained and chopped
3. 1/2 cup sun-dried tomatoes, chopped
4. Lemon dressing (made with lemon juice, olive oil, garlic, salt, and pepper)
5. Salt and pepper to taste (optional)

*Calories: Approximately 280   Protein: 7g.   Fat: 12g.   Carbohydrates: 35g.   Fiber: 6g.*


## Watermelon and Feta Salad

*Prep: 10min.     Cooking: 0min.     Serves: 4*

*Instructions:*

5. In a large mixing bowl, combine the cubed watermelon and crumbled feta cheese.
6. Sprinkle freshly chopped mint leaves over the watermelon and feta mixture.
7. Drizzle balsamic reduction or balsamic glaze over the salad.
8. Gently toss the ingredients until evenly coated.
9. Serve immediately as a refreshing side dish or appetizer.

*Ingredients:*
1. 4 cups cubed watermelon
2. 1/2 cup crumbled feta cheese
3. Fresh mint leaves, chopped
4. Balsamic reduction or balsamic glaze

*Calories: Approximately 110   Protein: 4g.   Fat: 3g.   Carbohydrates: 20g.   Fiber: 1g.*

# Salads

## Tuna Salad

*Prep: 15min.       Cooking: 10min.       Serves: 4*

*Instructions:*

1. In a large mixing bowl, combine the drained tuna, cannellini beans, halved cherry tomatoes, and thinly sliced red onion.
2. Prepare the olive oil-lemon dressing by whisking together olive oil, lemon juice, minced garlic, salt, and pepper in a small bowl.
3. Pour the dressing over the salad ingredients and toss gently until everything is well coated.
4. Season with salt and pepper to taste, if desired.
5. Chill in the refrigerator for at least 30 minutes before serving to allow the flavors to meld.
6. Serve chilled as a satisfying main dish or hearty side salad.

*Ingredients:*
1. 2 cans (5 oz each) tuna, drained
2. 1 can (15 oz) cannellini beans, rinsed and drained
3. 1 cup cherry tomatoes, halved
4. 1/2 red onion, thinly sliced
5. Olive oil-lemon dressing (made with olive oil, lemon juice, garlic, salt, and pepper)
6. Salt and pepper to taste (optional)

*Calories: Approximately 280   Protein: 22g.  Fat: 12g.  Carbohydrates: 20g.    Fiber: 6g.*

## Zucchini Ribbon Salad

*Prep: 10min.       Cooking: 0min.       Serves: 4*

*Instructions:*

7. Use a vegetable peeler or mandoline to thinly slice the zucchinis into ribbons.
8. Place the zucchini ribbons in a large mixing bowl.
9. Add the lemon zest and toasted pine nuts to the bowl.
10. Gently toss the ingredients together.
11. Sprinkle the crumbled feta cheese over the salad.
12. Drizzle with olive oil.
13. Season with salt and pepper to taste, if desired.
14. Serve immediately as a light and refreshing salad.

*Ingredients:*
1. 2 medium zucchinis, thinly sliced into ribbons (using a vegetable peeler or mandoline)
2. Zest of 1 lemon
3. 1/4 cup pine nuts, toasted
4. 1/2 cup crumbled feta cheese
5. Olive oil for drizzling
6. Salt and pepper to taste (optional)

*Calories: Approximately 120   Protein: 4g.  Fat: 9g.*
*Carbohydrates: 6g.    Fiber: 2g.*

# Salads

## Beet Salad

*Prep: 15min.    Cooking: 45min.    Serves: 4*

*Instructions:*
1. Preheat the oven to 400°F (200°C).
2. Scrub the beets and trim off any greens. Wrap each beet individually in aluminum foil.
3. Place the wrapped beets on a baking sheet and roast in the preheated oven for about 45 minutes, or until they are tender when pierced with a fork.
4. Once the beets are roasted, let them cool slightly, then peel off the skins and dice them.
5. In a large mixing bowl, combine the diced roasted beets and arugula.
6. Prepare the walnut dressing by whisking together walnut oil, balsamic vinegar, Dijon mustard, honey, salt, and pepper in a small bowl.
7. Drizzle the dressing over the beet and arugula mixture and toss gently to coat.
8. Sprinkle crumbled goat cheese over the salad.
9. Season with additional salt and pepper to taste, if desired.
10. Serve immediately as a vibrant and flavorful salad.

*Ingredients:*
1. 4 medium-sized beets, roasted and diced
2. 4 cups arugula
3. 1/2 cup crumbled goat cheese
4. Walnut dressing (made with walnut oil, balsamic vinegar, Dijon mustard, honey, salt, and pepper)
5. Salt and pepper to taste (optional)

*Calories: Approximately 250   Protein: 8g.   Fat: 18g.   Carbohydrates: 18g.    Fiber: 4g.*

## Cauliflower Tabbouleh

*Prep: 20min.    Cooking: 0min.    Serves: 4*

*Instructions:*
8. Rinse the cauliflower and remove the leaves and core. Cut it into florets.
9. Using a food processor, pulse the cauliflower florets until they resemble rice-like grains. Alternatively, you can grate the cauliflower using a box grater.
10. Transfer the riced cauliflower to a large mixing bowl.
11. Add the diced cherry tomatoes, diced cucumber, chopped parsley, and chopped mint leaves to the bowl.
12. Prepare the mint dressing by whisking together olive oil, lemon juice, minced garlic, salt, and pepper in a small bowl.
13. Pour the dressing over the cauliflower and vegetable mixture, and toss until everything is well coated.
14. Season with salt and pepper to taste, if desired.
15. Serve immediately as a refreshing and nutritious salad.

*Ingredients:*
1. 1 medium head cauliflower, riced
2. 1 cup cherry tomatoes, diced
3. 1 cucumber, diced
4. 1/2 cup fresh parsley, chopped
5. 1/4 cup fresh mint leaves, chopped
6. Mint dressing (made with olive oil, lemon juice, minced garlic, salt, and pepper)
7. Salt and pepper to taste (optional)

*Calories: Approximately 120   Protein: 5g.   Fat: 7g.   Carbohydrates: 15g.    Fiber: 6g.*

# Salads

## Shrimp Salad

*Prep: 15min.     Cooking: 5min.     Serves: 4*

*Instructions:*

1. Heat a skillet over medium heat and add a bit of olive oil.
2. Season the shrimp with salt and pepper if desired, then add them to the skillet.
3. Cook the shrimp for 2-3 minutes on each side until they turn pink and opaque.
4. In a large mixing bowl, combine the cooked shrimp, diced avocados, and arugula.
5. Prepare the citrus dressing by whisking together lemon juice, orange juice, olive oil, Dijon mustard, honey, salt, and pepper in a small bowl.
6. Drizzle the dressing over the salad ingredients and toss gently until everything is well coated.
7. Adjust seasoning with salt and pepper to taste, if needed.
8. Serve immediately as a light and flavorful salad.

*Ingredients:*

1. 1 pound shrimp, peeled and deveined
2. 2 avocados, diced
3. 4 cups arugula
4. Citrus dressing (made with lemon juice, orange juice, olive oil, Dijon mustard, honey, salt, and pepper)
5. Salt and pepper to taste (optional)

*Calories: Approximately 320   Protein: 25g.   Fat: 20g.   Carbohydrates: 15g.     Fiber: 8g.*

## Artichoke and Olive Salad

*Prep: 10min.     Cooking: 0min.     Serves: 4*

*Instructions:*

23. In a large mixing bowl, combine the halved artichoke hearts, pitted olives, and thinly sliced red onions.
24. Prepare the herb dressing by whisking together olive oil, red wine vinegar, Dijon mustard, minced garlic, dried herbs, salt, and pepper in a small bowl.
25. Drizzle the dressing over the salad ingredients and toss gently until everything is well coated.
26. Adjust seasoning with salt and pepper to taste, if needed.
27. Serve immediately as a flavorful and satisfying salad.

*Ingredients:*

16. 1 medium head cauliflower, riced
17. 1 cup cherry tomatoes, diced
18. 1 cucumber, diced
19. 1/2 cup fresh parsley, chopped
20. 1/4 cup fresh mint leaves, chopped
21. Mint dressing (made with olive oil, lemon juice, minced garlic, salt, and pepper)
22. Salt and pepper to taste (optional)

*Calories: Approximately 160   Protein: 2g.   Fat: 14g. Carbohydrates: 10g.     Fiber: 5g.*

# Salads

## Kale Salad

*Prep: 15min.     Cooking: 0min.     Serves: 4*

*Instructions:*

1. In a large mixing bowl, combine the thinly sliced kale leaves, chopped and toasted almonds, and pomegranate seeds.
2. Prepare the tahini dressing by whisking together tahini paste, lemon juice, water, minced garlic, salt, and pepper in a small bowl. Adjust the consistency with more water if needed.
3. Drizzle the tahini dressing over the salad ingredients.
4. Using clean hands, massage the dressing into the kale leaves for a minute or two to help tenderize them.
5. Season with salt and pepper to taste, if desired.
6. Serve immediately as a nutritious and flavorful salad.

*Ingredients:*
1. 1 bunch kale, stems removed and leaves thinly sliced
2. 1/2 cup almonds, chopped and toasted
3. 1/2 cup pomegranate seeds
4. Tahini dressing (made with tahini paste, lemon juice, water, garlic, salt, and pepper)
5. Salt and pepper to taste (optional)

*Calories: Approximately 250   Protein: 9g.   Fat: 18g.   Carbohydrates: 20g.   Fiber: 6g.*

## Sicilian Orange Salad

*Prep: 10min.     Cooking: 0min.     Serves: 4*

*Instructions:*

6. Arrange the orange slices on a serving platter.
7. Scatter the thinly sliced red onions and pitted olives over the orange slices.
8. Drizzle olive oil over the salad.
9. Season with salt and pepper to taste, if desired.
10. Serve immediately as a refreshing and vibrant salad.

*Ingredients:*
1. 3 large oranges, peeled and sliced
2. 1/2 red onion, thinly sliced
3. 1/2 cup olives (such as Kalamata or green olives), pitted
4. Olive oil for drizzling
5. Salt and pepper to taste (optional)

*Calories: Approximately 120   Protein: 2g.   Fat: 7g.   Carbohydrates: 15g.   Fiber: 4g.*

# Salads

## Mushroom Salad

*Prep: 10min.    Cooking: 10min.    Serves: 4*

*Instructions:*

1. Heat a skillet over medium heat and add a bit of olive oil.
2. Add the sliced mushrooms to the skillet and sauté for 8-10 minutes, or until they are golden brown and cooked through.
3. In a large mixing bowl, combine the sautéed mushrooms and arugula.
4. Prepare the balsamic dressing by whisking together balsamic vinegar, olive oil, Dijon mustard, honey, minced garlic, salt, and pepper in a small bowl.
5. Drizzle the dressing over the salad ingredients and toss gently until everything is well coated.
6. Sprinkle grated Parmesan cheese over the salad.
7. Adjust seasoning with salt and pepper to taste, if needed.
8. Serve immediately as a savory and satisfying salad.

*Ingredients:*
1. 1 pound mushrooms (such as cremini or button), sliced
2. 4 cups arugula
3. 1/4 cup grated Parmesan cheese
4. Balsamic dressing (made with balsamic vinegar, olive oil, Dijon mustard, honey, garlic, salt, and pepper)
5. Salt and pepper to taste (optional)

*Calories: Approximately 180    Protein: 7g.    Fat: 12g.    Carbohydrates: 15g.    Fiber: 3g.*

## Roasted Red Pepper and Almond Salad

*Prep: 15min.    Cooking: 15min.    Serves: 4*

*Instructions:*

7. Preheat the oven to 400°F (200°C).
8. Place the whole red bell peppers on a baking sheet and roast in the preheated oven for about 15-20 minutes, or until the skins are charred and blistered.
9. Remove the roasted peppers from the oven and let them cool slightly. Peel off the skins, remove the seeds, and slice the peppers into strips.
10. In a large mixing bowl, combine the roasted red pepper strips, toasted and chopped almonds, minced garlic, and chopped fresh parsley.
11. Drizzle olive oil over the salad and toss gently until everything is well combined.
12. Season with salt and pepper to taste, if desired.
13. Serve immediately as a flavorful and nutritious salad.

*Ingredients:*
1. 2 large red bell peppers, roasted, peeled, and sliced
2. 1/2 cup almonds, toasted and chopped
3. 2 cloves garlic, minced
4. 1/4 cup fresh parsley, chopped
5. Olive oil for drizzling
6. Salt and pepper to taste (optional)

*Calories: Approximately 200    Protein: 6g.    Fat: 16g.    Carbohydrates: 12g.    Fiber: 5g.*

Made in the USA
Monee, IL
02 June 2024

59287207R00063